Saint Nicholas of Myra: The Life and Legacy of Who Became the Inspiration for Santa Claus

By Charles River Editors

A 19th century depiction of Saint Nicholas

About Charles River Editors

Charles River Editors is a boutique digital publishing company, specializing in bringing history back to life with educational and engaging books on a wide range of topics. Keep up to date with our new and free offerings with this 5 second sign up on our weekly mailing list, and visit Our Kindle Author Page to see other recently published Kindle titles.

We make these books for you and always want to know our readers' opinions, so we encourage you to leave reviews and look forward to publishing new and exciting titles each week.

Introduction

Saint Nicholas

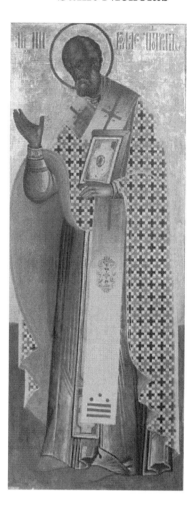

A Russian icon of Saint Nicholas

Christmas is the most important holiday of the year. After the corresponding days that exalt the national pride of each country, such as Independence Day in the United States, Victory Day in Russia, or Bastille Day in France, it's December 25 that articulates the life, the work and the economy in much of the world, including many non-Christian countries. Since ancient times, the beginning of winter has been the occasion for most people to eat, drink, dance, and get together to beat the drum and take a break.

Especially since the 20th century on, the days adjacent to the holiday have become an occasion to do big business. The winter season is the most solid stimulus for the economy - more than any fiscal package - since the incomes of families, spending, credit, and consumption in all productive sectors are significantly increased. In the United States alone, Christmas sales are estimated to generate $3 trillion.

One of the most important figures constantly brought up during the Christmas season is Saint Nicholas, despite the fact most people know little about him. In the 21st century, Saint Nicholas (or as people often refer to him, "Jolly Old Saint Nick") has been reduced to a pretend, adorably portly grandfather-type, a visual often accompanied by a fleet of magical reindeer and a bustling workshop staffed by endlessly cheerful elves. Most assume, quite understandably, that Saint Nicholas was the fount of inspiration that Santa Claus' myth weavers steadily drank from over the centuries. While this is accurate to some extent, it is important to remember that the parallels between Saint Nicholas and the present-day Santa Claus marketed by mass media are actually quite limited.

Santa Claus is a man with many monikers – Kris Kringle, Father Christmas, Papai Noel, among others – and is perhaps the most iconic and internationally recognized personality in recent history. Pop culture enthusiasts know to trace Santa's roots to Saint Nicholas, and it's widely accepted that Coke manufactured the contemporary image of Santa embraced by the world today. On both counts, they are only partially correct, because in reality, Santa is a colorful amalgamation of different figures who appear in various countries' folk stories across a wide range of centuries.

For starters, despite centuries of unabashed whitewashing, science has confirmed that Saint Nicholas, as his birthplace should suggest, was not white, nor was he excessively overweight. In the early 2000s, teams of researchers acquired copies of x-rays and logs of measurements originally compiled by scientists of Nicholas's skull in 1950, in the hopes of examining its framework in further detail. In 2004, a facial anthropologist at the University of Manchester, Dr. Caroline Wilkinson, succeeded in producing a forensically reconstructed 3D model of Nicholas's face; the reconstruction was refined in 2014. In both reconstructions, which captured Nicholas around the time of his death, his skin is olive-toned. It seems that he did sport a full beard, but it was untamed, scraggly, and silvery. He was balding and had benign, but forgettable features, with slightly protruding ears, brown eyes the shape of almonds, and small, sunken cheeks. And whereas Santa is, to most young ones, deceptively tremendous in both height and girth, more so when pictured with his tiny elves, Nicholas was roughly 5'6. Then there are the scientists who insist that he was shorter, and that his height was considerably below average, at just about 5'0.

What is arguably the most curious component of these reconstructions, however, is Nicholas's misshapen nose, which bears signs of struggle and friction now completely absent from the squeaky-clean image of Santa Claus. Furthermore, though both Santa and the saint are thought of as inimitably patient and in perpetually good spirits, realistically speaking, the elderly Nicholas would have most likely been somewhat crotchety and wretchedly miserable. In the years leading up to his death, Nicholas suffered from chronic arthritis that affected his pelvis and spine, a terrible physical pain that only worsened with time. He was also hounded by dreadful headaches and migraines, which arose from the bone thickening on his skull.

As this all indicates, the details in Nicholas's life have been stretched, then scrubbed away and replaced with softened truths and entirely fabricated traditions. As a result, this internationally celebrated figure has become more fiction than fact. However, when historians peel back the superficial layers of whimsy and caricatural perkiness swathed around his name, an image arises of a far more complex and fascinating character who did more than kick off the timeless tradition of gift-giving. Nicholas was not just a seasonal gift-giver, but a philanthropist who dedicated his life to helping the disadvantaged. He was not just a beloved bishop, but a fierce defender of the faith who remained undaunted in the face of persecution. To brand him a pious and God-fearing individual would be a massive understatement – indeed, he was, to those around him, the definition of a walking divinity, and an unrivaled miracle-worker sent straight from Heaven.

Saint Nicholas of Myra: The Life and Legacy of the Ancient Christian Bishop Who Became the Inspiration for Santa Claus looks at what his life was like, and how he served as the historical inspiration for Santa. Along with pictures depicting important people, places, and events, you will learn about Saint Nicholas like never before.

Saint Nicholas of Myra: The Life and Legacy of the Ancient Christian Bishop Who Became the Inspiration for Santa Claus

About Charles River Editors

Introduction

    A Gift Like No Other

    Working Wonders

    Guardian of All

    Saint Nicholas's Final Years and Posthumous Miracles

    Saint Nicholas Crosses Europe

    Jolly Old Saint Nicholas

    Online Resources

    Further Reading

Free Books by Charles River Editors

Discounted Books by Charles River Editors

A Gift Like No Other

"It was pride that changed angels into devils; it is humility that makes men as angels." – attributed to Saint Augustine

In the late 3rd century, Theophanes and Nonna (or Johanna) were an extremely devout and affluent Christian couple who lived in the picturesque port town of Patara, situated on the Mediterranean coast of Anatolian Lycia, now the southern coast of Turkey. To those on the outside, the one blessing they seemingly lacked was trivial, but Theophanes and Nonna were willing to part with their multiple beehive houses, their sprawling farmland, and all their wealth for the sake of this single blessing in question: a child to call their own.

The couple endeavored to fill this gaping hole in their lives for a long time, perhaps even three decades according to some. They dutifully visited their local church – their second home – all 365 days of the year, where they bowed their heads and immersed themselves in their prayers for hours on end. Each and every prayer was concluded with a heartfelt plea for a child, but their prayers were left unanswered.

When it seemed that all hope was long gone, Nonna, then in her late 40s or early 50s, was granted her only wish. In the year 270 CE (some say 280), Theophanes and Nonna welcomed their first and only son, a baby boy they christened Nicholas. Nicholas was the namesake of his uncle, a well-respected abbot of a monastery in Xanthos and the future archbishop of Myra. His uncle blessed and baptized the newborn just a few days after his birth.

Nicholas, a name of Greek origin meaning "victor of people," was a traditional, yet relatively uncommon name, but the name held special significance, particularly to those on the paternal side of his spiritual family. Nicholas, after all, was the name of one of the first men appointed deacon in Jerusalem. Like his uncle – one of the most prominent religious pillars of the community – and the other great Nicholases before him, young Nicholas, his family believed, was destined to bring victory to the Christian people.

The magnitude of the couple's wealth varies according to the source. Some portray them as inordinately opulent landowners and business owners with various properties, rolling swathes of land, an army of servants, and an impressive array of donkeys, cows, chickens, and other farm animals. Other biographers describe them as an adequately successful family who lived in a relatively spacious hut with a handful of servants. Author Vincent A. Yzermans, in *Wonderworker: The True Story of How Saint Nicholas Became Santa Claus,* described the family as "devoted Christians, not so poor as to be scorned by others, but neither so rich as to be boastful; they had enough to support themselves and still give to the poor."

Either way, it is clear that Nicholas was a privileged child who had what he needed. Even so, he would be taught to prioritize God above all others, and to put himself last. Never would

Theophanes and Nonna allow Nicholas to take anything for granted, because they sincerely believed that their manifold possessions were handed to them from above. They became even more convinced of this fact when Nicholas came into the picture, and his birth only heightened their determination to raise a passionately prayerful young man who would do nothing but good unto others, just as God was so very good to them.

As it turned out, there seemed to be no need to inculcate in him the importance of God, nor goodwill. If anything, his knowledge of this came from a young age, and as a child, he showed a preternatural sense of self-discipline. Most days, the unusually quiet and well-behaved infant drank from his mother's breast obediently, but when Wednesdays and Fridays rolled around, Nicholas would only accept a modest amount of milk at a certain hour. The infant, his biographers imply, was apparently aware of the concepts of Holy Wednesday and Good Friday without ever having been introduced to them, and he was mindful enough to fast on these days. Some say he refused his mother's milk altogether until after his parents completed their evening prayers.

When Nicholas was around the age of 7 or 8, a private *grammaticus*, or grammarian, was employed to guide him through his formal education. His intelligence was immediately noted by his instructor. That being said, Nicholas appeared to close himself off to all secular subjects, though he was more than competent in reading, writing, arithmetic, and typical studies. All his interest was instead invested in his lectures on philosophy, theology, and Scripture.

Nicholas was equally inhibited when it came to his social life. He did not care for drawing or coloring, nor was he type to roll around in the dirt. Instead, he chose to curl up in his favorite corner at home with his battered religious books, which he reportedly began to read at the age of 5.

During his adolescence, he avoided most others his age, specifically those who indulged in alcohol and reckless carousing, eschewing their worshiping duties at the house of God. Likewise, he steered clear of all women outside of his family and his church. He deliberately avoided eye contact with any female on the street, and he interacted with girls only when absolutely necessary, so as to circumvent all carnal temptations. Indeed, he was so resolved to live a life of pure austerity that he even abstained from listening to and playing non-religious music, and he avoided engaging in temporal entertainment as a whole, a far cry from the jingle bell-ringing and animated caroling traditions representative of Christmas today.

By choice, Nicholas spent the better part of his time conversing with God, and committing all Ten Commandments and Scripture to memory. While others in his privileged position gorged on delectable spreads and drank on a daily basis, Nicholas ate modestly, and he spent every other day fasting in the name of the Lord. He shared few things in common with those his age, and he would rather chant, pray, and socialize with the monks at his uncle's monastery, which he visited almost daily.

The inexplicable nature of his conception confirmed to Theophanes and Nonna that Nicholas would be a special child, but never in a million years could they have imagined the true depths of his powers. Legend has it that Nonna, who was gravely ill and teetering on the brink of death in the months leading up to the birth of Nicholas, was instantly cured upon his long-awaited arrival. Before the flush of a healthy glow could return to Nonna's cheeks, Nicholas, who had been placed in the small basin on the foot of the bed, astounded both women in the room when he supposedly hoisted himself onto his feet like a newborn calf, no more than a minute after his birth. He stood for only a few seconds before wobbling and collapsing into the water in a fit of giggles, but the event was remarkable all the same.

Weeks later, Nicholas did it again. The attendees of his baptism, performed by his uncle Nicholas, gasped in unison, some dropping to their knees, as the robust infant seized the edge of the baptismal font and pulled himself up. He refused to be scooped out of the water, and this time, stood for three hours straight, which was apparently the child's homage to the Holy Trinity. The infant's composure and his abstinence from tantrums, as well as his bypassing of the volatility and impulsivity often associated with emotional teenagers, also confounded those around him.

The mysterious, but striking occurrences that shadowed young Nicholas became even more inscrutable and spectacular with time. When he was 8 or 9, Nicholas left the home of his *grammaticus* one afternoon and stumbled upon a sickly old woman seated on the curb, sniffling over what appeared to be her shrunken hand. The child paused and furrowed his brows, as if listening intently to a voice in his head, before approaching the bashful woman. Without so much as a greeting, he cupped her withered hand, squeezed his eyes shut, and prayed vigorously, eventually ending his impromptu prayer session with the sign of the cross. The woman opened her mouth to thank the boy for the kind gesture, but all that sounded was a yelp of surprise. She watched in disbelief as a bright glow enveloped her atrophied appendage; by the time it subsided, her hand had become whole again.

This was an important milestone in his now budding life as a wonder-worker. While he had previously been the mere subject of miraculous circumstances, this is believed to be the first-ever miracle performed by Nicholas. Still, this wonder-worker could do nothing about the personal tragedy that was soon to unfold.

Nicholas was in his teens when both Theophanes and Nonna succumbed to complications stemming from the plague. Though his parents managed a large fishing fleet, among a handful of other similarly thriving businesses, they were altruists who spent the bulk of their time doing charity work. They had been serving a group of indigents ill with the crippling disease, and as such, they contracted the pestilence themselves. Early sources claimed it was the Plague of Cyprian, the terminal plague of the era, that claimed the lives of Nicholas's parents. The plague, named after its chief chronicler, St. Cyprian of Carthage, was so dreadful that Cyprian mistook the contagion as an indication of the world's approaching end. Cyprian wrote, "The kingdom of God, beloved brethren, is beginning to be at hand." No sum of gold was enough to keep the pestilence at bay, as evident by its casualties. In addition to countless nobles, the plague took the lives of not one, but two emperors: Emperor Hostilian in 251 CE and Emperor Claudius II Gothicus in 270 CE.

The symptoms recorded by Cyprian were horrific, to say the least: "As the strength of the body is dissolved, the bowels dissipate in a flow; a fire that begins in the inmost depths burns up into wounds in the throat... the intestines are shaken with continuous vomiting... the eyes are set on fire from the force of the blood... as weakness prevails through the failures and losses of the bodies, the gait is crippled or the hearing is blocked or the vision is blinded..."

Nicholas watched helplessly as his parents endured these torturous symptoms and the terrible disease eventually consumed them. Still, his unfaltering faith remained intact, another testament of his piety.

Now that he was an orphan, Nicholas received a hefty inheritance and numerous properties upon the death of his parents, but he had no interest in spending even a single coin of his parents' money. Shortly afterwards, he vacated and sold the family home, and he moved into Uncle Nicholas's monastery. In the company of his new guardian and the monks – his only friends – Nicholas processed his grief through extensive prayer binges and studying Scripture.

The older Nicholas was delighted by his nephew's religious zest. The younger Nicholas may have been several years or even decades younger than the monks and other fellow churchgoers, but these folks respected him and viewed him as a spiritual leader of sorts, often presenting to him questions regarding the faith and its doctrines. About a year or two into his relocation, Nicholas was appointed the official reader at Mass, and shortly after that he was inducted into the priesthood. Priestly responsibilities aside, Nicholas served as his uncle's personal assistant, and he was entrusted with the guidance of the church-going flock. Bishop Nicholas made the following remarks at his nephew's ordination: "I see, brethren, a new sun rising above the earth and manifesting in himself a gracious consolation for the afflicted. Blessed is the flock that will be worthy to have him as its pastor, because this one will shepherd well the souls of those who have gone astray, will nourish them on the pasturage of piety, and will be a merciful helper in misfortune and tribulation."

Nicholas was eager to live up to everyone's expectations. His sermons, as earnest as they were impassioned, moved every soul that heard them, and the words inspired listeners to not only spread forth the word of God, but to do good in their communities. The most effective part of his pedagogy was his resolution to live by example; not only was he an untiring prayer machine, but he never turned down anyone who sought his advice or aid. Moreover, he sold the family home and every last one of his possessions, dedicating the entirety of his inheritance to the destitute and the afflicted. He made it a point never to reveal his identity, or to call attention to his good deeds, for he felt that it would promote vanity and take away from the selfless gesture.

The most renowned of Nicholas's charitable accomplishments is a tale often referred to as "Saint Nicholas and the Three Impoverished Maidens," or "Saint Nicholas and the Three Purses," which Christians claim ignited the Christmas gift-giving tradition.

Roughly a year or so into his priesthood, Nicholas learned of (supposedly through a divine vision) a wealthy Pataran businessman who had abruptly gone bankrupt. The unnamed man, the father of three beautiful maidens, was inconsolable over the loss of his hard-earned fortune, so much so that he began to toy with the idea of selling off his daughters to a nearby brothel. Nicholas, who was greatly repulsed by the man's intentions, was committed to putting a stop to this idea immediately. Later that evening, he placed 300 gold coins into a handkerchief-satchel and tossed it into the open window of the man's home, which fell snugly into one of the woolen stockings that had been left by the fire to dry overnight.

Gentile da Fabriano's Renaissance-era painting of Saint Nicholas and the three maidens

The man discovered the satchel in the stocking the following morning, and he was predictably elated by the gift left behind by the unidentified Good Samaritan. His previous plan was scrapped, and instead, he paid a matchmaker to arrange a union between his first daughter and the son of an honorable nobleman.

The following morning, the father found another purse of gold in the same stocking by the fireplace, and this time he used the funds to ensure a safe and respectable future for his second daughter. In most accounts, the Samaritan and the beneficiary never crossed paths, but some versions of this tale describe a brief exchange. On the third evening, it is said, the father guarded the fireplace, awaiting the arrival of the secret donor. As soon as the third purse swished into the stocking, the father sprang to his feet and dashed out the door, intercepting the flustered Nicholas. The following dialogue is lifted from the biography penned by the 9th century historian Michael the Archimandrite, as translated by Professor John Quinn of Hope College in Michigan: "Ah, Nicholas, it is you!" the father exclaimed. "If our common master, Christ, hadn't stirred your goodness, we would have long ago destroyed our own lives by a shameful and destructive livelihood. But as it is, the Lord has saved us through you, most blessed one, and rescued us from the filth of immorality. And so we ought, like a debt, to give thanks to you all of our days, because you stretched out a hand of help to us and caused the poor to rise from the ground and raised the destitute up from a dunghill through your generous and truly wonderful gift!" Nicholas took the father's hand in his and acknowledged his gratitude, but he humbly entreated him to keep his identity and deed under wraps. He said, "You must thank God alone for providing these gifts in answer to your prayers for deliverance."

Not only did this oft-repeated tale spark off an international tradition still upheld to this very day, his protection of the young daughters is why he is now regarded as the patron saint of children and vulnerable "marriageable maidens" around the globe.

A few weeks later, Bishop Nicholas set out on his annual pilgrimage to Jerusalem. In his absence, the ecclesiastical flock was left in the care of the younger Nicholas. Upon the bishop's return, Nicholas requested a leave of absence for himself so that he, too, could embark on his first pilgrimage. The bishop, who was deeply appreciative of the diligence his nephew put into his duties, gladly granted his consent.

This is where the timeline gets a little hazy. In certain accounts, Nicholas only ventured out to the Holy Land after decades of priestly service and charity work, around 312 CE. In accounts related by other chroniclers, Nicholas was somewhere between his late teens or in his mid-20s when he undertook the religious excursion.

Whatever the case, Nicholas climbed aboard an antique, but still-functioning Egyptian vessel alongside other pilgrims as the captain set sail for the Holy Land. As the glowing orb of the sun began to sink towards the horizon, Nicholas's eyelids began to sink, too, lulled to sleep by the pungent scent of salty seawater and the soothing sound of the waves lapping the side of the boat.

Alas, the serenity that rocked him to sleep was nowhere to be found in his dream. An agonizingly vivid nightmare placed Nicholas aboard the same ship, but without the sailors and the other passengers traveling with him. Perplexed, he roamed the eerily empty vessel, his calls for help unreciprocated. Suddenly, the clouds began to swirl, and the pitch-black sky was illuminated by a frightening cluster of lightning bolts that turned the canvas an ominous shade of violet. Then came the torrential downpour and the powerful, wheezing gusts of wind. Nicholas held onto the side of the ship so as not to be thrown overboard, and he was struggling desperately to keep himself upright on the slippery floorboards, but an indescribable, pacifying warmth washed over him. His poise remained unimpaired, even when Satan – in the form of a blood-red, horned, winged beast – emerged from the black waters and began to climb onto the ship.

When Nicholas awoke the next morning, he relayed the divine message to the sailors of the ship. "A dreadful storm approaches," said Nicholas. "But do not fear, for God will protect us."

The sailors glanced up at the clear, cloudless sky, and with raised eyebrows, prepared to patronize the first-time voyager, but before they could do so, the sky immediately darkened, as if someone had dimmed the lights, followed by howling gales and rainfall that not only threatened to blow the ship off course, but overturn it altogether. Chaos erupted on the ship.

As the panicking passengers scrambled about on the boat, the sailors lowered the masts and cried out to Nicholas, begging him to pray for their safety. Nicholas, who was already calling out to God, ordered everyone around him to remain put, but one defiant sailor shimmied up the main mast to tighten the ropes in the hopes of preventing the fixture from toppling and irreversibly fracturing the deck. Unfortunately, on his way down, he slipped and landed headfirst on the deck, snapping his neck.

All those aboard the ship, excluding Nicholas, screeched in shock. The latter, however, fell to his knees and prayed, and within minutes, the storm had passed. But that was not the end of Nicholas's miracle. He then hovered over the dead sailor and prayed for his revival, which was instantly granted to him. There was a loud crack as the sailor's neck magically snapped back into place, and a chorus of gasps from the crowd as the sailor sat up, "as if he had only been asleep." Sailors and passengers alike lavished praise and gratitude upon Nicholas, but again, the modest priest pleaded with them to keep his feats a secret.

At last, the pilgrims arrived at Jerusalem. Nicholas was enraptured by the opportunity to walk where Christ had trodden, to nourish himself with the same food that Christ ate, and above all, to pray where Christ had worshiped. He also took to the welcoming, hospitable locals who offered up their homes to the pilgrims.

Late one evening, Nicholas made the trek to what was then the only church left standing in Jerusalem, the Church of the Room of the Last Supper. It took him several hours to navigate Mount Zion in the dark with no map, so it's easy to imagine his disappointment when he finally reached his destination only to see the farrago of chains and locks bolting the front doors shut. As Nicholas started to turn on his heel, the chains and locks disintegrated, and the front doors swung open, as if pushed open by invisible hands. He ducked into the church, and at once, he "fell to the ground in thanksgiving."

In the days that followed, Nicholas journeyed around Jerusalem, stopping at every sacred place "connected with the earthly service" of Christ. He fell so deeply in love with the area that he began to contemplate settling down in Jerusalem for good, but his plans were thwarted by the Lord, who visited Nicholas in another dream. "You must return to Lycia," God instructed him. "I have other plans for you there."

Naturally, Nicholas complied. He quickly wrapped up his pilgrimage tour, briefly stopping at Golgotha, Bethlehem, and the Holy Sepulcher before sailing back to Patara. On his way back home, he predicted another storm, and once again, he spared the lives of all on board with the power of prayer.

Working Wonders

"Children, I beseech you to correct your hearts and thoughts, so that you may be pleasing to God…Let us therefore strive to preserve the holiness of our souls and to guard the purity of our bodies with all fervor…" – attributed to Saint Nicholas of Myra

While some assert that he heard the spectral voice of God just a week or two into his pilgrimage, prompting his immediate return to Lycia, others say he traveled to Bethlehem and enrolled in a monastic community that dwelled in an assemblage of nearby caves. Here, the ascetic reportedly remained for three years. Not only did the solitude allow him to worship for several hours or days on end without interruption, it also provided him with the time to put his own thoughts to paper. He is rumored to have composed a few short manuscripts, perhaps regarding his interpretations of his favorite Biblical verses, or a journal in which he logged the divine revelations he received and the miracles he performed. Unfortunately, no copies of his original literature have survived.

Given his new lifestyle, the ascetic limited his visits to the outside world. As such, he made certain to exude goodwill and spread unto others the word and love of God on his rare trips into town. On one occasion, he encountered an elderly gentleman, supposedly drowning in debt and unable to feed his family, peddling a selection of rugs on the side of the road. To the delight of the vendor, Nicholas purchased three rugs from him, and insisted upon paying triple the price tag. On his way back to the caves, Nicholas stopped by the vendor's home, returned the merchandise to his baffled wife, and proceeded on his way back to the outskirts without ever providing his name or an explanation.

Nicholas is also believed to have performed a few miracles during his time in Bethlehem. One day, the monk chanced upon a beggar limping along the side of a road, dragging his deformed, wilted leg behind him. Without a second thought, Nicholas allowed the beggar to climb onto his back and carried him all the way back to the monastery. There, he rubbed the beggar's legs with holy oils and prayed for his recovery. The beggar rose from the ground, his previously paralyzed limb fully healed.

In other accounts, Nicholas only embraced the ascetic lifestyle when he returned to Lycia. With the consent of his uncle, Bishop Nicholas, the aspiring hermit entered the Monastery of Holy Sion, another monastery owned by his uncle, located in the fringes of the town. Neighbors gossiped about the seemingly fanatical religious ardor of the newly-tonsured monk, but their insults rolled off Nicholas like glue on rubber. Nicholas, they said, often quoted one of the Psalmists in response: "I have chosen rather to be an outcast in the house of my God."

The monks at Holy Sion, on the other hand, were overjoyed to have the astute and compassionate, yet strong-willed young brother on board. Nicholas himself was happy to be among them, for the introvert at heart craved a quiet life defined only by worship, contemplation, and personal reflection. But once again, Nicholas received irrefutable proof that this was not the path that God had paved for him. The Lord made this clear to him in another dream, saying to him, "Nicholas, if you desire to be vouchsafed a crown from me, go and struggle for the good of the world. [The Holy Sion] is not the vineyard in which you shall bring forth the fruit I expect of you; but turn back, go in to the world, and let my Name be glorified in you."

It pained Nicholas to part from the comfort he found in austerity, but as a faithful servant of the Lord, he did precisely as he was told. He packed the bare essentials in a small bindle and headed north, eventually wandering into Myra, Lycia's main metropolis.

At this time, the vibrant city of Myra was teeming with life and constant activity, but the adaptable Nicholas persevered. While he was scandalized by the paganism, impropriety, and moral turpitude that prevailed in the city, he found consolation in the fact that he was as much a stranger to the locals as they were to him. Nicholas neglected to bring any form of currency with him, for he was confident that God would provide everything that he needed. He had no contacts in this foreign city, and he lived as a pauper, scrounging for scraps of abandoned food and sleeping on the cold, hard floor of an abandoned church.

However, with God on his side, Nicholas would not remain a pauper for long. John, the bishop of Myra and archbishop of Lycia, was suddenly struck by an illness that claimed his life just days later. Following the archbishop's untimely death, the remaining bishops of Lycia convened in Myra at once to discuss the selection of a new bishop for the capital city. A few sound candidates stepped forward, but the prospective bishops argued amongst themselves and were unable to come to an agreement. In the end, one of the senior bishops presented his proposal: "The election of a bishop to this throne is not up to the decision of people, but it is a matter of God's direction.

It is proper for us to say prayers so that the Lord Himself will disclose who is worthy to receive such rank and be the shepherd of the whole land of Lycia."

That evening, the eldest and wisest of all the bishops was visited by God in a dream. In some accounts, the unnamed bishop heard a sonorous, but authoritative disembodied voice, and in others, he saw a "man in an image of light." "Arise early tomorrow morning, before the crack of dawn, and proceed to the church," the voice ordered. "Take care to watch the doors. Before the *matins* (the first prayer service of the day), a man will enter my house, and you will receive him. This is My choice; receive him with honor and install him as archbishop; the name of this man is Nicholas."

The elderly bishop did as he was instructed. About an hour before the start of the *matins,* the doors swung open, and in stepped an unassuming, disheveled young man. The bishop was dubious, but still, he confronted the gentleman and requested his name. "My name is Nicholas," the young man replied. "I am the servant of thy holiness, Master." The bishop replied, "Nicholas, servant and friend of God. God came to me in my slumber last night, and entrusted me to deliver to you this message: for your holiness, you shall be bishop of this place!"

The elderly bishop revealed the good tidings to his peers, who only then began to trickle into the church. Soon, word spilled out to the streets. Locals left and right buzzed with excitement and filed towards the church themselves, eager for a peek at the divinely appointed bishop. The following quote, translated by author William J. Federer, was proclaimed by the elderly bishop to the congregation: "Brethren, receive your shepherd whom the Holy Spirit Himself anointed, and to whom He entrusted the care of your souls. He was not appo9inted by an assembly of men, but by God Himself. Now we have the one that we desired, and have found and accepted the one we sought. Under his rule and instruction, we will not lack the hope that we will stand before God in the day of His appearing and revelation."

In some accounts, Nicholas was appointed bishop of Myra in the year 317 CE, meaning he was anywhere between 37-47 years of age. Other chroniclers, referencing his nickname, "Boy Bishop," insist he was far younger, perhaps around 30 years old, or that he may have even been in his 20s.

Even with what appeared to be the full-fledged support of the citizens and clergymen of Myra, the diffident Nicholas, who spent the first half of his life dodging the spotlight, was reluctant to assume the post. The only reason he ultimately accepted the position, like every major decision made in his life, was divine intervention. According to Saint Methodius, a few days prior to the death of Bishop John, Nicholas received another vision from above. In this vision, Nicholas, standing in the middle of an empty field, watched as Christ Himself descended from the heavens. Smiling, Christ handed to him a gilded Bible adorned with pearls and gems. Then, Theotokos – the Blessed Mother of Christ – materialized before him and draped over his shoulders a shimmering *omophorion* (the vestments sported by bishops in Lycia).

However it happened, Nicholas's new subjects – clergymen and laymen alike – held their new bishop in high regard, for he was to them a messenger and agent handpicked by the omnipotent God. One well-intentioned, but careless mother, however, was about to be presented with indisputable proof.

On the day of Nicholas's consecration, one young mother who had forgotten about the event prepared to bathe her toddler. Before she began to rummage around for some soap, she hauled the metal tub unto a fire, so as to keep the bathwater warm. That was when the cathedral bells began to toll, signaling the start of the consecration. In her trance-like state, the mother leapt to her feet and hastened towards the cathedral, promptly forgetting about her infant in the tub.

The young woman entered the cathedral, but only barely, for the church and the square around it was packed with just about everyone in the city. Still, she remained patient, and she stood in the winding queue stretched out before the bishop's seat. At long last came her turn for a blessing, but as soon as she saw Nicholas, it hit her, and the light on her face instantly vanished.

"Oh, Bishop Nicholas!" the mother cried, her wet face contorting with worry. "In my haste to attend your consecration, I neglected to remove my child from his tub."

Nicholas reached for the mother's hand before she could even complete her thought and bowed his head in prayer. "Do not be distressed," Nicholas assured her after the prayer session. "Your son is unharmed. Now, go with God."

Nicholas was right. The frantic mother returned home, coughing and crying miserably as she cut through the daunting billows of dark smoke, only to find her infant giggling and splashing around in the tub. She removed her baby from the tub, held him tight, and fell to her knees, praising God and Nicholas's name.

This, his chroniclers say, was the first miracle Nicholas performed as a bishop. It was at this stage that Nicholas grudgingly decided to omit the anonymity from his charitable acts and miraculous deeds. His promotion to bishop came as no coincidence; by voicing his convictions and openly showcasing his generosity for others, he could better impel his subjects to follow in his footsteps.

Guardian of All

"...Tell us every fault and failing;

We will bear thy keenest railing,

So we sing, so we sing:

Thou shalt tell us everything!" – Mary Mapes Dodge, "The Festival of Saint Nicholas" (1865)

Emperor Diocletian's hatred of Christians was evident ever since he rose to power in 284 CE, but in the year 303, the persecution of Christians rose to a new level. Nicholas, the bishop of the most affluent city in Lycia, was among those targeted by name, and as such, he was shackled and thrown into an excruciatingly shallow and lightless cell already congested with other Christians. It is said that the bishop remained behind bars for close to half a decade, and about a year into his stay, he was placed in solitary confinement, where he remained for the duration of his imprisonment.

On top of the starvation, lack of sunlight, and solitary loneliness, Nicholas was dragged out of his cell several times a week and made to endure numerous forms of barbaric torture. They whipped him with nail-studded scourges, wrenched off his nails one at a time, and twisted his flesh with blazing-hot iron pliers, but the resilient Nicholas persisted, refusing to renounce his faith.

It was only after the Edict of Milan, published by Emperor Constantine in 313 CE, that the persecution of Christians lifted and the prison sentences imposed by the former emperor were annulled. Christians who boldly refused to disavow Christ walked free and proceeded to flourish in the harmonious environment provided by the tolerant Constantine, but for Nicholas, this freedom was relatively short-lived. In 325, more than 300 bishops hailing from lands both near and far convened in the city of Nicaea, which was hosting an ecclesiastical conference now referred to as the "Council of Nicaea." The forum conducted debates on a variety of topics, predominantly concerning potential plans for expansion and new methods on affirming one's faith. The most stirring of these debates, however, were those centered on heresy. Arius, an Alexandrian presbyter and the founder of Christian Arianism, was the most controversial name on the docket.

Nicholas's seat in the front row provided him with a full view of the floor. When it came his turn to address Arius, the normally composed Nicholas shocked his peers by raising his voice to such an extent that the whole room seemed to rumble. The combative Arius retorted with greater volume and fervor, so much so that the increasingly agitated Nicholas became sorely fed up with his evasion of questions and his incessant hijacking of the conversation. In the midst of one of Arius's garrulous speeches, Nicholas got up, crossed the room, and slapped Arius on the cheek. Other accounts dismiss the open-handed slap, instead asserting that Nicholas's fist landed cleanly on Arius's right ear.

A medieval Greek icon depicting Saint Nicholas slapping Arius

Apart from the ringing in his ears, and perhaps a bruised ego, Arius was unharmed, but the law was clear. It was illegal for anyone – even bishops – to strike a man of the cloth, let alone such a high-ranking member of the community. Nicholas was apprehended by his fellow bishops, who hesitantly disrobed him, placed him in cuffs, and locked him in an underground cell.

Nicholas spent the rest of the evening praying, and he was rewarded with a visit from the angels (in other accounts, Jesus and Mary). The next morning, the jailer, along with a company of bishops, came by Nicholas's cell, prepared to mete out his final punishment. To their astonishment, Nicholas was seated cozily in the corner of the cell, fully dressed in his bishop's robes with his Bible open in his lap. The chains that had been bandaged around his wrists just hours ago lay in a neat coil next to the door of the cell.

When it was confirmed that Nicholas had been alone throughout the night, Emperor Constantine ordered the release of the bishop at once. Some biographers claim that this was yet another accomplishment in his portfolio of miracles, while others insist that it was his peers who conspired to free him. As the story goes, a number of other priests present claimed to have been concurrently smitten by the same vision. Christ and the Blessed Mother, they said, demanded that they restore Nicholas's bishopric status at once and to retract whatever punishment they had in store for him. Nicholas, the apparitions insisted, acted "not out of passion, but extreme love and piety." Saint Methodius wrote of the affair, "Thanks to the teaching of Saint Nicholas, the metropolis of Myra alone was untouched by the filth of the Arian heresy, which it firmly rejected as a death-dealing poison."

Katie Chao's picture of an ancient bust of Constantine

Once Nicholas was reinstated as bishop, he continued on his quest against paganism and false Christianity. He was strongly opposed to the reverence the local traditionalists displayed towards the virgin goddess of fertility, Artemis, once the most highly venerated deity in all of Lycia. It was his greatest fear as bishop that the locals would revert to their old worshiping habits, which included the vile practice of animal and human sacrifices. As such, it seemed only logical to dismantle all these pagan worshiping places, thereby eliminating the temptation and idolatry for good.

Not even Ephesus' Temple of Artemis, often lauded as the most breathtaking structure in Lycia and one of the Seven Wonders of the World, was spared. Philon of Byzantium, a Greek engineer from the 3rd century BCE, described the great temple: "[There is a hidden inner courtyard and] a great pagan altar, bigger than all others in height and width. I have seen the walls and Hanging Gardens of ancient Babylon, the statue of Olympian Zeus, the Colossus of Rhodes, the mighty work of the high Pyramids, and the tomb of Mausolus [sic]. But when I saw the temple...rising to the clouds, all these other wonders were put in the shade..."

A reconstructed model of the temple

The historic significance of the mighty temple was of no concern to Nicholas. One afternoon, the young bishop grabbed an iron hammer and set out on a rampage of pagan temple and shrine destruction, starting with the glorious Temple of Artemis. With all the strength he could muster, Nicholas clubbed the columns and smashed the porcelain statue of the goddess into hundreds of pieces. So thorough was his work that by the end of the destruction, even the foundations of the centuries-old establishment had been torn out of the ground.

In other accounts, such as the version penned by the 10th century saint and hagiographer, Symeon the Metaphrast, Nicholas does not lift a finger, but instead destroys the temple via prayer. In his book, *Vita Per Metaphrasten*, Symeon the Metaphrast wrote, "As soon as the saint began praying, the altar collapsed, and the statues of the idols fell down, like leaves of a tree when a strong wind blows in autumn. The demons who inhabited the place left, but protested to the saint amidst their tears: 'You have been unjust to us. We did you no harm, and yet you send us away from our home. We had made this our home, while these misguided people adored us, and now where can we go? And [to this] the saint replied: 'Go to Hell's fire, which has been lit for you by the devil and his crew.'"

More importantly, Nicholas was a staunch defender of the people. Not long after his second stint in prison, a band of soldiers was dispatched by Emperor Constantine to Phrygia (more precisely, Frigia Adaifalorum) to quash a budding revolt. Among these soldiers were three high-ranking officials named Ursus, Eupoleonis, and Nepotianus. The soldiers got on a boat and set sail for Phrygia, but due to a lack of wind, they drifted to the town of Andriake in Lycia, about three miles or so from Myra. Once they were safely anchored, the soldiers split into two groups - one would venture into town and gather food and other provisions, while the rest would remain and guard the ship. A conniving company of thieves spying from afar caught onto the arrival of the stranded soldiers and wasted no time in exploiting the situation. As soon as the latter group of soldiers – Ursus, Eupoleonis, and Nepotianus included – dipped into the lake for a quick bath, the thieves pilfered their uniforms and launched a major looting spree.

Unsurprisingly, the mob that later formed at Phrygia's main plaza, Placomatus, demanded retribution. The commotion at Placomatus, they say, was so deafening that even the citizens of Myra could hear the furor. Perturbed, the bishop traveled to the plaza in Andriake. He was spotted by the broken group of troubled soldiers and quickly flagged down. The following dialogue is taken from Charles W. Jones' *Saint Nicholas of Myra, Bari, and Manhattan*.

"Where do you come from," Nicholas wanted to know. " – and on whose business do you come, and for what reason do you come?"

"We are peaceful," the soldiers replied. "Our most benign emperor sent us to engage in battle with some lawbreakers, and we are on our way. Pray for us , most holy father, that we may prosper on our journey, [for] three of our brothers have been wrongly condemned to death by Eustathius the Praeses (governor of Andriake). Please, you must not let them die for a sin they have never committed."

And with that, Nicholas mounted one of the army's stallions and sped towards Byrra, where they were to be beheaded. When he arrived, the executioners were wielding their glinting swords above the prisoners, each head enclosed in a linen sack, lowered in resignation. The bishop hopped off his horse and charged towards the executioners, grunting loudly as he pushed his staff against the executioners' swords.

"The righteous are bold as a lion!" Nicholas bellowed, his eyes flashing. "Put down your swords and release these men at once, for they are not the thieves you seek!"

Taken aback by the fierce confrontation, the executioners complied. Not only did they set down their swords, they sawed off the ropes that tethered the prisoners' hands together and released them. The bishop then sidestepped the grateful soldiers, ignored the mixture of cheers and jeers from the crowd, made a beeline for Pretorium, and stormed into the chambers of the governor, Eustathius. Eustathius, who at this point, had already been informed about the failed execution, implored for the bishop's forgiveness, but Nicholas would have none of it.

"Sacrilegious blood shedder!" Nicholas roared. "How dare you confront me, apprehended in so many and such evil acts! I will not spare or forgive you, but will let the mighty emperor Constantine know about you – how many and how serious are the sins which you have been discovered in, and in what fashion you administer your princely prefecture!"

Wholly frightened, Eustathius continued to grovel at Nicholas's feet, and he attempted to shift the blame unto the other officials. "Be not wrathful with thy servant," the governor pleaded. "[I] speak the truth, that I am not the guilty one, but the heads of state, Eudoxius and Simonides."

But Nicholas, who was aware of the 200 pounds of silver Eustathius accepted for the executions beforehand, would not be swayed. He replied, "It is not Eudoxius and Simonides who did this, but silver and gold."

Nicholas's refusal to entertain the shallow apologies of the corrupt official, as well as his assault on Arius, are infrequently mentioned, but they remain important chapters in his life all the same, for they humanize a character that is too often marketed as flawless and unerring.

***Saint Nicholas Saves Three Innocents from Death*, by Ilya Repin (1888)**

Little did the soldiers know that they would require Nicholas's services again shortly. Once their mission at Phrygia was complete, the soldiers returned to Constantinople. In a show of their admiration for the soldiers' tenacity and ensuing triumph, the citizens of Myra prepared for them a splendid homecoming parade, followed by an even more colorful feast.

The attention showered upon the soldiers incited the envy of the elderly army general, who now regretted his choice to stay behind and hold down the fort. Thus, he approached a dishonorable prefect named Ablabius and instructed him to lay a new set of false charges upon the same three soldiers who had previously been unjustly condemned to death. In return, Ablabius would receive 1,700 pounds of gold. The morning after the banquet, Ablabius paid a visit to Constantine and relayed to him the following message: "Most pious lord, a great…conspiracy has been formed against Your Potency by the officers of the army who were sent to [Phrygia]. For I learn as a fact that they have engaged themselves to rise up against Your Clemency. They make pretense that they are acting in [sic] your behalf while they work for money and bribes and create high honors for themselves. When I learned of this, I could not keep silent…Now, immediately, if it please Your Clemency, act!"

Constantine was conflicted, and he was somewhat skeptical about the serious accusations leveled against these soldiers, but to appease the restlessness, he ordered the arrest of the three soldiers. Still, Ablabius was not contented, for every minute the convicted continued to breathe, the likelihood of his lies unraveling remained. Again, he bowed down before the emperor, and he further embellished his lies. He warned Constantine, "My lord, behold how those men whom you ordered to be incarcerated...live on in prison, developing their intrigues throughout the imperial rule of Your Amplitude and Potency! If you do not act now, my lord, they will soon have your head and seize your throne!"

Upon being wrongly sentenced to death for the second time, Nepotianus clasped his hands in prayer and urgently cried out to the heavens. "Lord God of Nicholas, have mercy upon us...just as Thou did with [us when we] were iniquitously and unjustly adjudged to death in Lycia, when Thou did save them, now in like fashion, save us." Alongside him, Ursus and Eupoleonis prayed with identical ardor, only they directed their pleas to the bishop: "[Bishop Nicholas], servant of Christ, though you be far from us, bring your intercession...nearer to us, and your behest to Thy Lord God and Our Lord Savior Jesus Christ. Intercede for us that we be rescued from iniquity, and the death-bearing tempest, that we may be deemed worthy to come and adore the most holy tokens of thy paternity!"

Curiously, it was not Jesus who made an appearance in the dreams of both Constantine and Ablabius that evening, but a livid Bishop Nicholas with fiery, unblinking eyes and a chilling timber in his voice. He said to Ablabius, "Ablabius, stricken in neither conscience nor mind, rise and free those three men...whom you hold in custody, for they are innocent. Should you decide to disobey me and claim their heads tomorrow evening, I shall bear witness against you before the immortal King Christ, and you will fall ill and end as food for forms, and your whole family will perish evilly."

The following morning, Constantine ordered the release of the soldiers, and in their place, he filled the vacant cell with the wicked and unrepentant Ablabius. But before the soldiers departed, the emperor imparted to them one last set of instructions: "Now understand this – it is not I who have granted to you your life, but he whom you did invoke...Nicholas, to whom you are devoted. Cut the hair of your head, and don your proper uniforms. Then render thanks to him. And be charitable towards me." As one final gesture of remorse, Constantine gifted to them a chest filled with gilded Bibles, sacred chalices, a pair of ornate candles, and a patina – the platter used to serve the Eucharist – encrusted with twinkling jewels. The soldiers, twice rescued by Nicholas, made no protests. They traveled to Myra, where they distributed their belongings and the treasures to the poor. They then shaved off their hair, adopting the classic tonsure, and joined the local monastery, where they remained for the rest of their lives, all in the name of Bishop Nicholas.

Saint Nicholas's Final Years and Posthumous Miracles

"The giver of every good and perfect gift has called upon us to mimic God's giving, by grace, through faith, and this is not of ourselves." – attributed to Saint Nicholas of Myra

The final years of Nicholas's life were marked by more mystifying miracles and fantastic feats that demonstrated his genuine love for his flock.

As the legend goes, once upon a time, three little boys (brothers or neighbors, according to different accounts) were collecting whatever edible roots they could find in the parched earth, which had been desiccated by the famine. When their stinging, blistered fingers could pick no more, they reluctantly called it a day and headed off into town. Exhausted, dehydrated, and with their stomachs still rumbling, the knackered children ended up at the local butcher shop and rapped on the door with what little energy they had left. "Kind sir," said one of the boys when the butcher answered the door. "As the sun has now set, we are unable to find our way home. If you could please spare us some food and a space on your floor to sleep, we would be so very grateful."

The butcher eyed the children and grinned. "Why yes, boys. Come in – let us get you fed and rested."

Oblivious to the menacing tone of the butcher's voice, the children entered his shop. One by one, they were lured to the rear room with the promise of food, only to be strangled, hacked up into several pieces, and tossed into a large pickling tub. Some say that the butcher preserved the children's corpses in brine for a full 7 years before serving their flesh to unsuspecting customers. In most accounts, however, Nicholas learned of the gruesome murder that same evening in a dream. The next morning, an enraged Nicholas banged on the butcher's door with his crosier. Petrified by the look in the bishop's eyes, the butcher confessed immediately and led him to the crime scene. There, Nicholas placed his hand over the ghastly contents of the tub and prayed furiously under his breath.

"Rise up, children!" the bishop boomed. "Rise up, and go with the Lord!"

Miraculously, the children emerged from the seething amber-colored water, their limbs reassembled. "Hallelujah!" the children cried. "Give praise to Nicholas and Christ, our Savior!"

With that, the children strolled out of the butcher shop, good as new, and hurried home to their families. This, they say, is how Nicholas became the patron saint of students and barrel makers.

A depiction of Nicholas resurrecting the children

Of course, barrel makers are only some of the unlikely characters who came under Nicholas's swiftly growing patronage. 1,850 miles to the west, in a quaint, unmarked village in Italy, lived two brothers named Giuseppe and Alfredo. The brothers, like most of the villagers, were deprived and disadvantaged, and as such they were forced to rely on their cunning to provide for themselves. By their mid-teens, they had garnered a reputation as chronic career criminals who engaged primarily in theft. They targeted only the rich and committed other petty crimes, but they were crimes all the same.

Even so, deep down, they were good kids who respected their elders, and they often shared their loot with the underprivileged. Be that as it may, their widowed mother feared for their souls. She dedicated over an hour of prayer regarding her boys each evening, pleading for the Holy Spirit to wash over them and reverse their ill-fated habits. Eventually, God called upon

Nicholas and instructed him to appear to Giuseppe and Alfredo, apparently bestowing upon him the power of divine astral projection.

A day or two later, Giuseppe and Alfredo were foraging through the kitchen of a herdsman who was away for the night. After stuffing themselves with some bread and cheese, and washing down their finds with wine, the brothers found themselves a spot on the floor and drifted off to sleep, soon to be greeted by Bishop Nicholas of Myra.

Nicholas knew that a mere warning would not be enough to dissuade them from resuming their life of crime. In order to drive his message home, he took them on an illusory tour reminiscent of the journey that Ebenezer Scrooge embarked upon with the Ghosts of Christmas Past, Present, and Future. In short, the tour, which was designed to show the brothers the unseen repercussions of their crimes, concluded with the boys at the gallows and their heartbroken mother weeping in the crowd.

When the Italian brothers arose the next morning, they returned the valuables they pilfered from the herdsman and strode out the door changed men. Never again would they take what did not belong to them; instead, they started a proper business, from which they earned a modest, but sufficient, living. This, they say, is how Nicholas became the patron saint of thieves.

Nicholas's God-given powers, it seems, only evolved with time. Apart from resurrecting the dead, the bishop was Myra's resident exorcist. Grief-stricken parents summoned Nicholas to expel the wicked demons dwelling in their children's bodies, which he did with no more than his Bible, an aspergillum, and his trusty crosier. And demons were not the only evils he combated. If anything, the fabled bishop's abilities knew no bounds, for he could even tame literal beasts. As one such legend goes, Nicholas succeeded in subduing a vicious dragon that had terrorized a nearby town for centuries.

Nevertheless, the bishop's most momentous miracles were those that benefited not just one or two souls, but all of Lycia. Following a string of particularly poor harvests that devastated the region's food supply, the bishop prayed to God for an answer, and Lord informed him of an Italian merchant who was in the midst of loading his ship with a consignment of grain destined for Egypt. That evening, Nicholas revealed himself to the merchant in a dream. "Do not bring the grain to Egypt," said the bishop. "Instead, deliver the grain to Myra, and sell it there, where the people are in dire need of nourishment. Do this, and I pledge to you three gold coins."

When the merchant arose the next morning, he unclenched his fist, startled to find the three pieces of gold he had been promised. Thoroughly rattled and unwilling to defy what seemed to clearly be a message from the heavens, the merchant sailed to Myra and unloaded the grain there. Because of that intercession, the citizens of Myra were provided with enough grain to outlast the famine.

Another rendition of this tale has the bishop interacting with a merchant moored not in some Italian port, but in Andriake, the harbor closest to Myra. As the merchant carefully stacked bundles of wheat into the cargo of his ship – one in a fleet en route to Alexandria – he was approached by a pensive Nicholas. "Good sailor and servant of God," the bishop greeted him. "If you could part with just a small fraction of the cargo on each one of your vessels, to sell to the desperately hungry here, the Lord would be most pleased."

"I'm afraid there's nothing I can do," replied the merchant. "The cargo on these ships are meted and measured. I must deliver them all as is, for if I fail to do so, it is I who is left to answer for any shortage."

But Nicholas stood firm. "Leave it in the hands of God," he assured the merchant.

With a little more convincing, the merchant finally agreed to remove 100 bushels of grain from each of his vessels. As expected, the merchant had nothing to fear, for by the time the ships arrived at their destinations, the missing stock had been magically replenished. The citizens of Myra, along with the thunderstruck merchant, praised the masterly bishop and the generous heavens for the miracle. The wheat fed the citizens of Myra for two years; the leftover grain also served as seeds for many fruitful harvests.

Interestingly enough, not all of Nicholas's exploits were miraculous in nature. It is said that the bishop once traveled 300 miles to the heart of the empire, where he persuaded authorities to reduce the taxes paid by those in society's lower echelons.

On December 6, 343, the bishop laid his head to rest for the very last time. As winged seraphs surrounded him, he whispered, "I have hope in Thee, O Lord. Lord, into Thine hands I commend my spirit."

With a final exhale, the bishop's eyes fell shut, his soul ascending from his body to the glorious soundtrack of melodic trumpets and the euphonious voices of singing angels.

A few months later, the citizens of Myra constructed a church in Nicholas's honor and stored in it an exquisite coffin filled with the bishop's remains and other blessed relics. But despite the fact that the bishop was now deceased, the miracles have yet to cease. To begin with, just days after Nicholas was entombed, a clear, sweet-smelling liquid, now referred to as "manna," began to excrete from his bones. Anyone who comes into contact with this cryptic substance, it is said, is instantly healed from their ailments, be they physical or mental.

Remarkably, when the bishop's bones were exhumed in 1953, the linen cloth underneath the relics was reportedly drenched with manna, and this fragrant river continues to flow from his bones to this day. On the 9th of May each year, the Feast of the Translation of the Relics of Saint Nicholas, a Dominican priest is tasked with collecting the oily liquid in a glass vial, which he then uses to bless the attendees of a commemorative Mass held for the ancient bishop. The pleasant scent of the manna, which has often been compared to the smell of rose water, accounts for the saint's patronage of perfumers.

Of course, it should come as no surprise that the authenticity of the manna continues to be a matter of great dispute. It is lambasted by critics as an immoral sham propagated by the Church. Not only are these bottles of manna – now available in select gift shops – veritable cash cows, the riveting story behind the product only aids in furthering their agenda. In 2002, a Venetian church that claimed to be in possession of a vial of 12th century manna was dealt a humiliating blow when scientists, who collected a sample of the liquid for testing, discovered that the church elders were hoarding plain vegetable oil from the 1300s.

Regardless, when considering the kaleidoscopic catalog of miracles Nicholas supposedly performed from beyond the grave, it is not difficult to understand how the cult around him blossomed at such an exponential rate. In one story, a young Christian man borrowed a sum of money from his Jewish neighbor, and to seal the deal, he pledged to return the money on a sacred painting of Saint Nicholas. When it came time to collect payment, the Christian mendaciously insisted that he had already settled the debt. The Jew, however, who had anticipated such a stunt, presented to him the same painting of Saint Nicholas. If the Christian could swear on the image that the debt had truly been settled and emerge unscathed, he would consider the debt repaid.

Undaunted, the debtor hobbled over to the painting with his cane, laid his hand on the painting, and made the oath with an unabashed air of nonchalance. The creditor, therefore, had no choice but to allow the debtor to return home, as previously negotiated. Under the impression that he had been exonerated, the debtor bade the Jew a hearty farewell and turned on his heel, only to be knocked over by a cart that came careening out of nowhere. The debtor was somewhat scratched up, while his can had snapped in half, and out spilled the roll of coins that he had secretly tucked into its hollow center. The creditor received the money he was owed, and the debtor vowed never to repeat the stunt again.

There was also a tale about a married couple from a town in Eastern Europe. Like Theophanes and Nonna, the husband and wife longed for a child. Following an extended pilgrimage to Myra, where they paid tribute at all of the hallowed sites devoted to the fallen bishop, their prayers were finally answered. That coming winter, they welcomed a son on the 6th of December, the feast day of Saint Nicholas.

Sadly, their exultation was extinguished just days later, when a crew of thieves crept into the house, stole the newborn, and sold the child to a Muslim caliph as a slave. Day in and day out, the disconsolate husband and wife wept and prayed for the safe return or happiness of their only son. At long last, on the 6th of December, exactly a decade later, Saint Nicholas freed the boy from the chains of the Saracens and returned him to his gleeful parents.

Nicholas's cameos from the afterlife were not limited to phantasmic apparitions and unfathomable interventions. At times, the apparent shape-shifter disguised himself as man. In the Lombardie (now Lombardy) region of Italy lived a pious and honorable man with a young daughter. On the feast day of Saint Nicholas, he headed to the nearby cathedral to pay his respects, leaving his slumbering daughter behind. About half an hour after the father's departure, the young girl was awoken by a raucous knocking on the front door. The child had been taught to assist the needy whenever the opportunity presented itself, so when she peered out the window and saw a frail, elderly woman dressed in tattered rags armed with only an empty bowl, she opened the door at once and invited her in for some bread. Alas, as soon as the girl's back was turned, the beggar revealed her true form, transforming into none other than Satan. The devil lunged at the young girl from behind and throttled her until she flailed no more.

The father was crushed when he discovered his daughter's lifeless body, his guttural wails reverberating throughout the neighborhood. In the midst of his mourning came another knock on the door. The father brushed off his tears and staggered towards the door, where he found a different hungry pilgrim humbly requesting for scraps from his dinner table. Rather than send the pilgrim off to his neighbor, the father invited the pilgrim in and began to prepare for him a warm meal. The pilgrim – Saint Nicholas in disguise – was so moved by the kind father's unstinting magnanimity that after disclosing his true identity, he restored the man's daughter to life.

Saint Nicholas Crosses Europe

As the compelling tales regarding the bishop's life and miracles spread, the cult around him grew accordingly. By the year 450, there were numerous churches scattered throughout Asia Minor and Greece consecrated in his honor. 90 years later, Byzantine Emperor Justinian I ordered the construction of an extravagant cathedral in Constantinople (present-day Istanbul), which he then dedicated to Bishop Nicholas of Myra. By the dawn of the 9th century, Nicholas was the principal saint of the Eastern Orthodox Church.

In the year 842, Saint Methodius, then the Bishop of Constantinople, composed a biography (in Greek) revolving around the miracles and feats of Saint Nicholas, now considered one of, if not the oldest and most extensive of its kind. The glittering hagiography, an instant hit, was translated into Latin by John the Deacon some four decades later.

By the mid-800s, ecclesiastical authorities at the Cologne Cathedral in North Rhine-Westphalia, Germany were practicing what was then a newfound tradition of gift-giving during the feast day of Saint Nicholas. On the 6th of every December, the clergy distributed sacks of fruits, cookies, and other treats to the students enrolled at the cathedral school. They also sang hymns dedicated to the revered saint, which had been popularized just a decade or two earlier.

Many historians today credit Princess Theophanu, the future Empress Consort of the Holy Roman Emperor, with introducing the cult to the West. Her subjects' obsession with the saint, they say, started when the princess gifted the Saint Peter's Basilica in Rome a ravishing mosaic of Nicholas, depicted with a Bible ornamented with precious stones in one hand and his gilded crosier in the other. The mosaic was installed on the 14th of April, 972, the day that she wedded Emperor Otto II.

When Byzantine Emperor Alexios I Komnenos succeeded Emperor Nikephoros III Botaneiates in 1081, barbarians – capitalizing on the instability brought about by the transition of power – began to launch a series of attacks on Asia Minor, beginning with its coastal cities. Religious authorities at Myra were understandably disquieted by the attacks, more so when the barbarians began to penetrate metropolitan cities. The relics of the saint – at the time, still housed in Myra – were transferred to the second Church of Saint Nicholas within the locality for safekeeping, but the possibility of the brutal, but intuitive barbarians discovering the Church's most precious treasures was still far too high for their liking.

Six years later, miles away in Bari, Italy, a priest supposedly received a vision in which the bishop himself demanded to be removed from Myra. The following week, the priest marshaled three groups of sailors, provided them three separate ships, and instructed them to extract Saint Nicholas's remnants from its hiding place in Myra so that they could be safely guarded in Bari. Thus, in the spring of 1087, the sailors voyaged to Bari, where they soon found the second Church of Saint Nicholas. By then, the church had fallen to ruins and was inhabited by no more than four monks.

What transpired next is a matter of debate. In some accounts, the monks were beaten unconscious by the sailors, who then proceeded to make off with the chest of relics kept underneath the church. In most accounts, the sailors expressed to the monks their intentions, persuaded them to hand over only some of the relics, and even managed to convince two of the monks to return to Bari with them.

As the Italian soldiers pulled up to the Bari shores, they were greeted by the enthusiastic hurrahs of the crowds who had come to receive them. That afternoon, the saint's relics were paraded around in a procession that encompassed the entire city, and then displayed at the altar during the Mass hosted by the Church of Saint John the Forerunner and BaptiSaint Nicholas's skull and the bones of his hands were later encased in a pair of beautiful, handcrafted silver boxes, while the rest of the sacred remnants remained in Myra. On the 20th of May (in other sources, the 2nd of June), the silver boxes were later transferred to a new church established for Saint Nicholas, where they continue to be housed to this day.

Didier Descouens' picture of the Church of San Nicolò al Lido in Venice, which is said to house fragments of the saint's bones

The Basilica of San Nicola in Bari, where most of the saint's relics are said to be housed

In the centuries that followed, Christian sailors and maritime merchants, who also viewed Nicholas as their patron saint, continued to spin and spread tales about the bishop in faraway lands. As a result, European seaports saw a spike in churches dedicated to the saint. To accommodate the saint's popularity, which experienced a notable resurgence in the Middle Ages, metropolitan cities throughout Europe followed suit. By the end of the 15th century, Nicholas had become the patron saint of Sicily, Apuila, Athens, Lorraine, as well as Austria, Switzerland, Germany, Russia, Belgium, and the Netherlands, among other major European powers. Thousands of existing churches were also rebranded in the name of the bishop saint, including over 400 churches in England, 300 in Belgium, 34 in Rome, and 23 in the Netherlands.

The leaders of the Protestant Reformation made several significant attempts to flush away the memory and legacy left behind by the bishop saint, but Nicholas ultimately prevailed. Today, he is one of the most recognizable saints in the world. Moreover, the umbrella of his patronage is more prodigious than ever, a meandering list that includes children, orphans, scholars, sailors, merchants, grooms, haberdashers, judges, longshoremen, archers, brewers, pawnbrokers, thieves, bankers, laborers, travelers, paupers, marriageable maidens, students, captives, and victims of judicial mistakes. For the full list, one can consult the *Saint Nicholas Center*, an online database devoted to the saint.

Inevitably, given the passage of time and the exaggerated tales told about him, some question whether Nicholas was an actual person or simply a popular protagonist featured in the history of Church-manufactured propaganda? To start with, skeptics who value the integrity in science find it difficult to accept – and rightfully so – that miracles exist. The fact that the Church insists it was a mere man who produced said miracles, many of which defy the laws of science to an outlandish extent, only adds to the preposterousness of the equation. It also bears repeating that the earliest biographies of his life were written centuries after his death, mainly by avid followers of the saint.

On the other end of the spectrum, it is hard for some to completely discount the innumerable accounts of miracles that occurred after Nicholas's death, particularly those in recent years. Furthermore, there seems to be some scientific evidence that confirms the bishop's existence. Apart from the facial reconstructions produced by Dr. Caroline Wilkinson in 2004 and 2014, experts from Oxford University unveiled another pivotal piece of the puzzle in 2017. Oxford scientists Tom Higham and Georges Kazan tested a microsample of a bone fragment – most likely of Nicholas's pelvis – from the private collection of Father Dennis O'Neill. Following a number of radiocarbon tests, the scientists confirmed that the age of the bone fragment corresponded with the timeline provided by Nicholas's hagiographers. "Many relics that we study turn out to date to a period somewhat later than the historic attestation would suggest," said Higham. "This bone fragment, in contrast, suggests that we could possibly be looking at remains from Saint Nicholas himself." His partner, Kazan, added, "It is exciting to think that these relics, which date from such an ancient time, could in fact be genuine."

For a tentative, but more well-rounded conclusion to this open-ended mystery, one can refer to the theory of Dr. Adam English, a theology professor at North Carolina's Campbell University. In essence, Dr. English believes that Nicholas was real, to a certain degree. He more or less discredits the supernaturally charged feats and miracles of Saint Nicholas and reduces them to inspirational fables, but he also acknowledges that there is an often an overlap between the stories of two externally similar, but distinctive characters: Nicholas of Myra and Saint Nicholas of Sion, who died in 564 CE. Furthermore, he attributes the resurgence of the saint's popularity to the litany of plays about Nicholas of Myra produced throughout the Middle Ages, a form of entertainment known for exaggerating real events for dramatic effect.

In the library managed by Dominican friar Gerardo Cioffari, Dr. English found what he called "compelling clues of the saint's historicity." Of all the extraordinary events in the saint's life, English believes that the story of his rescue of the unjustly condemned soldiers – recounted by Michael the Archimandrite – is most credible. He explained, "It's a fascinating story, because in it we see Nicholas acting not simply as a Christian pastor or a religious leader, but as a social activist...[The story includes a] number of specific places, proper names rooted in history, and other clues that verify this as a legitimate historical account."

Jolly Old Saint Nicholas

Regardless of whether Nicholas actually existed, the impact that his story had on Christians is undeniable, and his influence on Christmas is even more widespread.

In the West, Nicholas was extolled as the guardian saint of all children. On this feast day, December 6, Christians venerated him by presenting gifts to their loved ones and neighbors. This tradition was reportedly practiced in Utrecht, the Netherlands, as early as 1163.

It is now believed that the practice was ignited by a lowly party of nuns from an unnamed French village. At first, they traveled only to the rundown shacks or sleeping places of penniless children, stealthily leaving behind small parcels of candy before vanishing into the night. As operations expanded, nuns began to slink into the unlocked doors of vacant homes, packing satchels of candy into the shoes of the well-behaved, and a single switch of willow into the boots of troublesome children. How these nuns kept track of delinquent children is unknown; one can only assume that some kind of collaboration between the parents and the nuns took place.

More often than not, the nuns preferred to remain anonymous. When asked about the source of these mysterious gifts, this was their only response: "It must have been Saint Nicholas!"

Not all the nuns delivered treats. On the morning of Saint Nicholas Day, poverty-stricken families awoke to baskets of bread and other foodstuffs, as well as packages of clothing, and at times, a few silver coins wrapped in rags. Occasionally, the nuns also lodged a single tangerine or apple (a rather costly fruit back in the day) into the heels of stockings and filled the remaining space with a medley of nuts.

The trend of giving gifts on Saint Nicholas Day eventually caught on with other regions in the Low Countries, spreading to Germany, Austria, Switzerland, and England, and even reaching Romania. The French nuns were permanently substituted with the visiting spirit of Saint Nicholas, painted as a rail-thin, wrinkled wraith dressed in a scarlet bishop's robe.

By the late 13th century, sweets and other treats were retired in favor of larger ornaments and novelties of special significance. This next phase of gift-giving, historians theorize, was prompted by the Catholic Church with the intention of incorporating the presents extended by the Three Magi in the story of the Nativity into the holidays. Enterprising vendors sought to capitalize on the new trend by erecting "Saint Nicholas markets," which were populated with vibrant stalls filled with toys, trinkets, and treats.

European royalty also began to partake in the gift-giving tradition. In 1377, the court subjects of France's King Charles V received gilded chalices filled to the top with myrrh, incense, and blocks of gold. On New Year's Day, subjects who could afford it presented their monarchs with another set of handsome gifts. Fortunately for these subjects, they did not leave empty-handed; instead, they walked out of the king's chambers with either a silver-gilt basin or a satchel of coins.

Although Saint Nicholas Day had become synonymous with generosity and gift-giving, he was still a far cry from the rosy-cheeked, happy-go-lucky Santa Claus of the 21st century. Children in the devoutly Catholic portions of Europe dreaded the winter arrival of the ghostly saint, for he was designed as a virtuous, but vengeful bogeyman who preyed on wicked children.

In Germany, there were two gift-bearers bound together by a "good cop, bad cop" dynamic: Saint Nicholas and his sidekick, Knecht Ruprecht (Farmhand Rupert). Rupert, wearing a dirt-brown (sometimes lace-white), hooded cloak edged with black fur, trawled the streets in the dead of the night, filling his gut with misbehaving children. In Switzerland and the Netherlands, Nicholas shoved bad children into the infinite space within his sack with all the care of a litter collector equipped with a trash picker. The pulsing sack of children was then dragged deep into the Black Forest, never to be seen again.

In certain parts of Austria, religious parents went even further to drive home the importance of proper conduct. On his feast day, the saint, garbed in full bishopric regalia, banged on the front door of wicked children, demanding to be let in. The panicking children made themselves scarce, curling up under the bed or inside of closets. Once the coast was deemed clear, they peeked out from their hiding spaces, only to be seized and hauled into the next room by the awaiting bishop. The bishop then loomed over the cowering children and swung the switches in his fist forward in one swift motion, stopping short just above the head of the sniffling child. Misbehave again, the bishop snarled, and he would be back the following year. Whether they were presents or rod-beatings, Saint Nicholas always delivered.

Teachers employed at Christian schools, particularly those affiliated with the saint, also began to expand on the tradition. Every 6th of December, they seated themselves behind their desks, dressed as the divine saint. One by one, the queue of pupils stepped forward to hear their verdict. Students with satisfactory to excellent grades and good deportment were rewarded with sweets or a bit of spending money. Those with substandard scores and poor conduct were made to stay after dismissal and beaten with birch rods.

These punishments had indeed become a principal constituent of the Saint Nicholas Day traditions, but the Roman Catholic Church reminded Christians not to lose sight of the celebration's paramount message. Demonstrating one's love for their children and one's appreciation for their exemplary behavior was well and good, but it was more important for the rich to share their wealth with the needy. As Ambrose of Milan, an associate of Saint Nicholas, once put it, "You are not making a gift of your possessions to the poor person. You are handing over to him what is his. For what has been given in common for the use of all, you have arrogated to yourself. The world has been given to us all, and not only to the rich."

While the concept of deliberately urging one's children to place their faith in a fictitious character might seem relatively strange or archaic to some, the aforementioned evidence indicates that this brand of trickery had no age. As time progressed, scheming parents across Europe continued to keep up the pretense, and they began to modernize the original traditions associated with Saint Nicholas Day. A 15th century Swiss author, Rudolf Hospinian, noted, ""It was the custom for parents, on the vigil of [Saint] Nicholas, to convey secretly presents of various kinds to their little sons and daughters who were taught to believe that they owed them to the kindness of Saint Nicholas and his train, who, going up and down among the towns and villages, came in at the windows, though they were shut, and distributed them."

The same sentiment is also found in a poem penned by 16th century German dramatist Thomas Naogeorgus:

> "...And when they every one at night
>
> In senseless sleep are cast
>
> Both apples, nuts, and pears they bring,
>
> And other things besides
>
> As caps, and shoes, and petticoats,
>
> Which secretly they hide,

And in the morning found, they say

That this Saint Nicholas brought..."

The momentum of the Saint Nicholas-inspired gift-giving movement began to decline in 1517, the dawn of the Protestant Reformation. Catholics were relentlessly chastised for their "undue" worship of the canonized, mainly towards the miracle maven Saint Nicholas. The Industrial Revolution, the rise of Puritanism in Europe, and criticism of the veneration of saints, which included special dedications to Saint Nicholas and St. Wenceslaus, overshadowed the feast in Europe. The Calvinist theologian Walich Sieuwertz wrote, "It is a foolish and pointless custom to fill children's shoes with all sorts of sweets and nonsense. What else is this but sacrifice to an idol? Those who do it do not understand what true religion is." In their *History of New York*, Edwin Burrows and Mike Wallace write that "since the Reformation, protestants dismissed Christmas as another artifact of Catholic ignorance and deception. Not only was the New Testament silent on the date of Christ's birth, they noted, but the Church had picked December 25 to coincide with the beginning of the winter solstice, [an] event traditionally associated with wild plebeian bacchanals and challenges to authority."

Martin Luther, the seminal leader of the Reformation, officially outlawed all festivities commemorating the saint in Protestant territories. That being said, Luther had no delusions about the ban he was enforcing, and he was well-aware of the furtive celebrations that would inexorably take place out of sight. In a bid to fill the gap of a celebratory figure during wintertime, Luther spun together the story of *Christkindlein*.

Christkindlein, otherwise known as "*Christkindl*," or simply "Christkind," directly translates into "Christ Child." Initially, *Christkindl* was depicted as a chubby, cherub-like Jesus in toddler form. German Christians, however, could not be sold on the idea of an infant, winged Christ flitting from house to house in the middle of winter, for no such story or mention of a gift-bearing Christ is referenced in the Gospel. To rectify this, a new character was manufactured. Henceforth, *Christkindl* was no longer Christ, but an androgynous, nameless baby angel with butterscotch-blonde ringlets, twinkling blue eyes, and fluffy golden wings.

The iconography of *Christkindl* differed in various parts of Protestant Europe, including territories in what is now Austria, Liechtenstein, Hungary, Switzerland, Slovakia, and the Czech Republic. In some versions, *Christkindl* was depicted as a young, wingless girl clothed in a hooded fur coat, trudging through dense blankets of snow. A deer was sometimes seen trotting alongside her, a hefty basket of toys and fruits balanced on his snout. Other times, *Christkindl* carried out the mission on her lonesome, pushing a wheelbarrow of goodies through curtains of falling snow.

Christkindl arrived not on the 6th of December, but on the 24th of the month, the last day of the Advent. Presents were neatly stacked underneath the *Weihnachtsbaum,* an evergreen tree adorned with lighted candles, now considered the precursor of the Christmas tree. As was customary during the time, Protestant parents advised their children against conspiring to catch *Christkindl* in the act; the gift-giving angel, they claimed, skipped the houses of nosy young ones. Only when they hear the toll of the bell (hooked up and operated by their parents) did they come rushing out of their rooms, making a beeline for the gifts under the *Weihnachtsbaum*.

Ironically, another legend attributes the invention of the Christmas tree, or perhaps the "Christianization" of the Yule log, to Martin Luther, who was supposedly walking through the snowy forest one Christmas Eve, saw the beautiful stars shining through the branches of a fir tree, and was so moved that he took one to his house to show his son the genuine Christmas message: that Christ was the light of the world. The origin of this unmistakably apocryphal tale is possibly a painting by an artist named C.A. Schwerdgeburth which shows the leader of the Reformation and his family sitting around a beautiful Christmas tree.

More variations of Saint Nicholas continued to crop up all over Europe in the centuries that followed.

16th century English diarist Henry Machyn recounted the enthralling Saint Nicholas Day celebrations that unfolded on the streets of London in the 1550s: "[People costumed in Nicholas' bishopric robes] went abroad in most parts of London singing after the old fashion...received among good people into theirh ouses, and had much good cheere [sic] as ever they had in many places..."

Interestingly enough, though the terms "Father Christmas" and "Santa Claus" are interchangeable in the United Kingdom today, the first Father Christmas and Saint Nicholas were not one and the same. The nameless forerunner of Father Christmas (named as Grandfather Christmas here so as not to cause confusion) made his first debut in the pagan lore and mid-winter customs of the ancient British peoples.

In spite of what his name might suggest, King Frost was the heralder of springtime – a towering, white-bearded figure draped in a floor-length, emerald-green cloak ornamented with a single wreath of ivy, holly, or mistletoe. When Britain entered the Anglo-Saxon period in the 5th century CE, the character of Grandfather Christmas was merged with that of "Saxon Father Time," also known as "King Frost," or "King Winter." Dawn Copeman of *Time Travel Britain* explained, "Someone would dress up as King Winter and be welcomed into homes, where he would sit near the fire and be given something to eat and drink. It was thought that by being kind to King Winter, the people would get something good in return: a milder winter. Thus, Father Christmas became associated with receiving good things."

The final ingredients that would complete the medieval Father Christmas came with the 11th century invasion of the Normans, who brought with them the stories of the legendary Saint Nicholas.

The earliest tangible reference to Father Christmas, however, is dated to a 15th century carol authored by the Rector of Plymtree, Richard Smart:

"Nowell, Nowell, Nowell, Nowell,

'Who is there that singeth so?'

'I am here, Sir Christëmas.'

'Welcome, my lord Christëmas,

Welcome to us all, both more and less

Come near, Nowell!'"

It was only then that Father Christmas became the embodiment of the spirit of Christmas. During the Tudor and Stuart eras, Father, Sir, and Captain Christmases were summoned to the late-winter parties and Christmas displays hosted by public establishments and in the spacious parlors of the upper class.

In 1638, Worcestershire-born dramatist Thomas Nabbes produced the first visual of the synthesized Father Christmas in his court masque, *The Springs Glorie*: a disheveled, rotund, and pipe-smoking old man with small, smiling eyes, and a whisker-and-beard combo the color of fresh-fallen snow, dressed in a "furr'd gown and cap." On Christmas Eve, Father Christmas galloped all over town on his donkey or mare, sneaking small presents into stockings and pillowcases dangling over the fireplace or on the headboards above sleeping children. As a token of their gratitude, children prepared for Father Christmas a slice of mince pie, accompanied by a tumbler of brandy.

Alas, halfway into the 17th century, ultra-conservative British Puritans who could no longer stomach the overindulgence and intemperate carousing linked to Christmas banned the holiday – along with Father Christmas – altogether. Even so, devotees continued to pay homage to Father Christmas while taking their operations underground. The character was quietly inserted into wintertime Mummers' Plays ("seasonal folk plays performed by troupes of actors known as "mummers" or "guisers"). The following is an opening line frequently used in such plays: "In comes I, old Father Christmas," the actor announced as he took center stage. "Be I welcome, or be I not? I hope old Father Christmas will never be forgot."

Besides these cult dramas, Father Christmas also made several cameos in the articles of back-alley newspapers. Authors of these newspapers in question referred to him as "Old Christmas," which was symbolic of the people's nostalgia towards the forbidden holiday. Pamphlets printed by enthusiasts and so-called "recusant Catholics" on the sly called for the return of Father Christmas. The following is a passage from one of these pamphlets: "Any man or woman, that can give any knowledge, or tell any tidings of an old, old, very old gray-bearded gentleman, called Christmas, who was wont to be a very familiar guest and visit all sorts of people, both poor and rich, and used to appear in glittering gold, silk and silver, in the court, and in all shapes in the theater in White Hall, and had ringing, feasts and jollity in all places, both in the city and the country, for his coming – whoever can tell what is become of him, or where he may be found, let him bring him back again into England!"

The prohibition on Father Christmas was eventually lifted, but it was only when Britain entered the Victorian Age that the Christmas spirit was reanimated in full swing.

Meanwhile, 323 miles to the east of London, Dutch children across the Netherlands patiently awaited the arrival of *Sinterklaas.* By the 17th century, trees were a common sight throughout northern Europe. An unidentified 35-year-old man who visited Strasbourg in 1605 left this description in his travel journal: "At Christmas time in Strasbourg people put up fir trees in their living room. Then hang roses cut in papers of many colors, 40 apples, wafer and goldplated (decorations)."[1] That said, this does not mean people were placing pine trees upright in the middle of a living room. In some parts of Austria and Germany, the tree was hung upside down in a corner of the room and decorated with apples, walnuts, and strips of colored paper. Others were nothing more than thick branches hung from windows and doors. There was still at least a century to go before the symbol took its present shape.

---

[1] *Deutsch: Denken, wissen und kennen.* Holt, Rinehart and Winston, 1966.

Around this time, historians can also trace the first mentions of *Sinterklaas* in Europe, an amalgamation of Saint Nicholas, Father Winter, and possibly Odin. It is not clear at what point the Christian bishop merged with the winter character and possibly with the Norse god, but most of the elements of the legend of *Sinterklaas* seem too foreign to any Christian tradition, even considering that the lives of the saints acquired fantastic traits during the Middle Ages. According to folklore, *Sinterklaas* rides through the heavens on a horse followed by a cohort of black or demonic helpers who inform him about human behavior. In other versions, *Sinterklaas* arrives in the villages accompanied by a black helper named Zwarte Piet (Black Pete), a diabolical character who inflicted corporal punishments on children or kidnapped them to take them to a place of torment.

A depiction of *Sinterklaas* and Black Pete

On the evening of December 5th, Dutch children pored over Scripture for hours on end prior to the advent of *Sinterklaas*, for the purpose of his visit was to catechize them on their biblical knowledge. It was absolutely essential that they pass the test with flying colors, for failure meant the irreversible damnation of their souls.

About five minutes before the arrival of *Sinterklaas*, the children of the household formed a tidy queue behind the front door. Following a short hymn exalting him for his unparalleled benignity, the door was cracked open. A withered hand reached in through the gap of the door and threw a handful of sweets down the hallway. Then, without warning, the door swung open, and in stepped *Sinterklaas*, usually played by a parent, relative, or neighbor.

The scowling *Sinterklaas* strode into the parlor and circled the children, the wine-red cape tied over his white bishop's alb fluttering behind him. After a lengthy strare, the jittery children were ordered to pull up a chair each. He then paced back and forth in front of them, rhythmically slapping a birch rod against an open palm as he quizzed them on random areas of the Bible.

"Who disobeyed God, and was, as a result, transformed into a pillar of salt?"

"What sea did Moses part?"

"Recite the 10 commandments!"

For every accurate answer, the children were rewarded with another handful of sweets (and at times, oranges). In contrast, each error was met with a hearty slap on the hand or the child's behind. Children who were unable to summon up even one correct answer were sentenced to an eternity in the blazing bowels of Hell. Children who failed two years in a row were crammed into *Sinterklaas*' filthy sack and prematurely dragged to Lucifer's lair.

Spanish Aragon conquered Bari, along with the rest of the territories within the Norman Kingdom of the Two Sicilies, in 1442. Holland followed suit when it allowed itself to become absorbed into the kingdom of the Spanish Hapsburgs a little over a century later. Shortly after the transition, Dutch Catholic bishops began to spend the summer in Spain, and the spirit of Saint Nicholas, they claimed, journeyed to the verdant Spanish countryside with them. At first, a major obstacle prevented *Sinterklaas* from breaking away from his duties – he could not peel his eyes away from the Dutch children, so as to keep his behavior log accurate and up-to-date. As such, *Sinterklaas* employed a young Moorish fellow named *Zwart Piet* (Black Pete) and tasked him with monitoring the children and updating the records in his temporary absence. Later, *Zwart Piet* began to accompany *Sinterklaas* on his gift-giving expeditions, carrying in his own satchel the birch rods for naughty and ungodly children.

Anthropology professor Benjamin K. Swartz, Jr. described the character of Black Pete in further detail: "In function, Black Pete serves as a Dutch non-pagan version of the German

Knecht Ruprecht (Farmhand Rupert)…a black sprite helping Saint Nicholas as a disciplinarian or children. Ruprecht 'appears in shaggy, sack on back…and rod in hand' in the 16th and 17th centuries…The English counterpart of *Knecht Ruprecht*, Robin goodfellow is documented as early as 1489, [and] had a loud laugh of Ho Ho Ho. Indeed, numerous supernatural 'little people' were associated with Saint Nicholas at this time in German folklore, contributing to his eventual elfin status and collaboration with elf helpers."

19th century Swedes, perhaps taking a page out of the book of the British Christians in the 1550s, took to the streets with dramatic and highly-colored parades aimed to elevate the Christmas spirit. Court subjects and servants from the retinue of King Oscar II – some faces coated in stage makeup and others concealed behind intricately detailed masks – sang Christmas carols and swung their baskets of gifts in tfheir arms. The arresting array of costumes was endless, ranging from royals and soldiers to sailors and spooky harlequins. The central figure of the Swedish gift-giving pantheon was *Julbocken,* a "Christmas goat" that first infiltrated the mainstream via *Petter och Lottas Jul* (*Peter and Lotta's Christmas*), published by author Elsa Beskow. The magical goat, most likely another derivative of *Knecht Ruprecht*, was portrayed as a mythical character who presented gifts and goodwill to well-behaved children.

The *Tomten* was another prominent character in the pantheon. *Tomtens* were tiny and tubby gnome-like creatures with curly white beards and pointed red caps who dwelt in the crawlspace of each Swedish home, protecting all the children and animals within the vicinity from evil spirits and other negative energy. Around mid-December, the *tomtens* relocated to the attic, the hollow space underneath staircases, and other nooks and crannies of the house. Once all members of the family were snugly tucked into their beds, the mischievous gnomes squirmed out of their hiding places and stowed loose treats and valuable trinkets into hard-to-find crevices, setting in place a sort of treasure hunt for the family.

If the family provoked the *tomten,* however, they retaliated. The family would then find themselves the targets of mild, but infuriating pranks (i.e., missing socks, gloves, toys, or the premature souring of milk), and they would be cursed with a spate of bad luck.

By the 1800s, the two characters had been fused into one: the *Jultomten,* also known as *Tomten,* or *Nisse. Jultomten* was a stern, no-nonsense shape-shifter who took on the form of a short, crooked-backed gentleman, clothed in a long, tattered coat. His basket of gifts was mounted on the back of his pet ram. On Christmas Eve, *Jultomten* pounded on every front door. "Have the children inside been good?" he boomed from the other side of the door. When *Jultomten* received confirmation from the parents of the household, he briskly slipped through the door and delivered the presents, supposedly darting in and out of the door in the blink of an eye.

To express their gratitude, children whipped up bowls of savory porridge and platters of almond and butter and left them by the main entrances of their homes. *Jultomten* could also be tided over with offerings of tobacco or liquor. Those who failed to do so were at risk of incurring the wrath of the pint-sized gift-giver. Not only would they receive the cold shoulder from the *Jultomten* the following year, they were subjected to cruel tricks and practical jokes.

Additionally, in Sweden and certain parts of Germany, people began to exchange gifts they called *"Yule-klapp"* as a kind of obeisance to Saint Nicholas. *Yule-klapp* were typically pendant necklaces, rings studded with precious stones, or some other glittering gift. The presents were swaddled in a silk cloth and placed in multiple boxes in increasing sizes, creating a Russian nesting doll effect. As dictated by tradition, the gift-bearer knocked on the door of the recipient's home, and when the recipient came to greet them, the gift-bearer hurled the *Yule-klapp* through the door and ran off as quickly as their legs could carry them, so as to keep their identity veiled.

The mingling of Saint Nicholas and Christmas customs over time only resulted in more charming traditions. In France, *Père Noël* (the French rendition of Saint Nicholas) was presented as a slender, elderly gentleman dressed in a baggy, hooded red robe trimmed with white fur. His presents were not lugged around in a sack, but instead, a *hotte*, a handwoven basket similar to those carried by grape harvesters. On the 24th of December, French children dusted off their boots and *sabots* (clogs chiseled out of wood), filled them with carrots and apple slices for *Père Noël's* donkey, Gui, and set them down by the fireplace. For *Père Noël,* they prepared a glass of fine wine or *Calvados*, the latter a type of apple or pear brandy produced in the Normandy region of France.

Contrary to popular belief, the mythical gift-bearer was not always a male figure. Take into account, for instance, Lady Befana of Italian lore. When the Three Wise Men ventured out from the Middle East in search of the newborn king, they relied on the Star of Bethlehem as their compass. Their extensive journey took them across numerous towns and countries, among them an obscure and unmarked town in Italy. The inhabitants of every village they chanced upon flocked towards them in throngs to escort them to their destination. When the magnetic Magi passed by the Italian village, all the villagers spilled into the streets and tagged along en masse, joining the wise men's fast-swelling cortege, except for one little old lady.

"Come quick!" her neighbors called out to her. "The Three Magi are here!"

"Do not wait for me," the old lady replied, waving them off with her broom. "There is plenty of housework still to be done, but I have no doubt I will finish before your departure."

The old lady continued to work around her house, sweeping, scrubbing, and cleaning, oblivious to the falling, then rising sun. When she finally completed her housework, she set down her broom and wiped her hands on the sides of her patchy dress, admiring the spotlessness of her own handiwork. Only then did she take heed of the piercing, pin-drop silence and the beam of early morning sunlight caressing her cheek. The old lady snatched up the gift box on the supper table and hobbled out the door, broom still in hand, but the villagers were long gone.

La Befana, as she has since been christened, has yet to complete her quest for the newborn king. Every year, on the 6th of January, she hops on her broomstick and flies across the continent, stopping at the home of every child along the way. She fishes one of the presents out of her basket, which she wears like a backpack, and shimmies down the chimney, stuffing a pile of knick-knacks in hand-knitted stockings or laying them under the Christmas tree. Still unable to locate the newborn king, she bestows a present upon every child in the hopes that she will finally find him.

When the story of Befana was first established sometime in the 13th century, children were ordered to stay in their beds. Those who flouted their parents' warnings, it is said, received a hard smack on their behinds from her broomstick. To thank Befana for her troubles, each family rustled up a platter of sandwiches and other finger-foods, accompanied by a glass of red wine.

Italian children spent the last week of December knitting stockings and composing wish lists, as well as letters addressed to Befana detailing their behavior over the past year. Well-mannered children could expect to find pretty dolls, handmade puppets, and wooden novelties in their stockings. Unruly children, on the other hand, received stockings stuffed with garlic, coal, and old onion bulbs.

Saint Nicholas' winged horse first touched down in the New World in the early 17th century, alongside the Dutch and German colonists that came to settle in North America. Few records have survived, but historians believe that the gift-giving traditions surrounding the magnanimous saint were first practiced by Dutch families, predominantly in New Amsterdam (now New York City). German, Belgian, and Polish colonists stationed in Pennsylvania may have also celebrated the feast day of Saint Nicholas.

On the 23rd of December, 1773, England-born James Rivington's *New York Gazetteer* published an article covering the Boston Tea Party. In it, he mentioned that clans of Dutch families had convened at a local tavern to honor Saint Nicholas: "Last Monday, the Anniversary of Saint Nicholas, otherwise called St. A Claus, was celebrated at Protestant Hall, at Mr. Waldron's; where a great number of the sons of that ancient saint celebrated the day with great joy and festivity." Rivington was, therefore, the first to publish an article in North America that mentioned Saint Nicholas and his feast day by name. As one can gather, he also made the first reference to "Santa Claus," identifying him as "St. A Claus," possibly a misspelling of the Dutch "*Sinterklaas.*"

Saint Nicholas disappeared from papers was not again chronicled until approximately 20 years later, when his traditions were resurrected by a New Yorker by the name of John Pintard. Pintard – a merchant, philanthropist, active Freemason, and secretary for the Academy of Fine Arts – hinted at his intrigue with Saint Nicholas in his private journal in 1793 and 1797, but it was not until the first years of the 19th century that he took his movement off paper.

Pintard

In 1804, Pintard became one of the 11 founders of the New York Historical Society, said to be the first museum in the state. Pintard recognized the importance of stockpiling and preserving journals, books, eyewitness accounts, and other records of their history, saving them from "dust and obscurity." The cynicism of these men had been hardened by their experiences during the American Revolution and the British invasion of New York City in 1776. They longed for simpler times and were distraught by the immorality and godlessness that seemed to define New York norms.

Saint Nicholas was unofficially adopted as the society's mascot, a personification of the sweet, uncomplicated days of yesteryear. In 1809, Pintard gave the following toast at the society's annual dinner celebrations: "To the memory of Saint Nicholas. May the virtuous habits and simple manners of our Dutch ancestors be not lost in the luxuries and refinements of the present time."

The impassioned mentions of Saint Nicholas that Pintard made at the dinner table were not lost on his family and friends. Eventually, most in his family grew weary of the subject and could only afford to part with lukewarm interest at best, humoring him with half-hearted replies. Two of Pintard's closest comrades, however, remained interested: Manhattan-based author Washington Irving and Episcopalian minister and part-time wordsmith Clement Clark Moore.

Irving

Moore

The inquisitive Irving first called attention to the figure in January 1808. That month, he wrote in *Salamagundi*, a literary magazine of his creation renowned for lampooning influential politicians, "The noted Saint Nicholas - vulgarly called 'Santa-Claus' – of all the saints in the kalendar [sic] the most venerated by the true Hollanders, and their unsophisticated descendants." The sarcasm dripping from the above excerpt is a common theme present in many of Irving's works, but they are at the same time, laced with clues that point to his unspoken, but genuine love for the winter season. He nade a second, more elaborate reference to Santa Claus in his satirical history book, *History of New York*. The book was published under the Dutch pseudonym of "Diedrich Knickerbocker" on the 6th of December in 1809, hence the manuscript's alternative title: *"Knickerbocker's History of New York from the Beginning of the World to the End of the Dutch Dynasty."*

In *History of New York*, Saint Nicholas was acknowledged as the patron saint of New Amsterdam and was described as a "jolly old Dutchman, nicknamed 'Sancte Claus', who parked his wagon on rooftops and slid down chimneys with gifts for sleeping children on his feast day."

In an effort to top the previous year's celebrations, Pintard commissioned artist Alexander Anderson to produce a delicately detailed woodcut illustration of Saint Nicholas, which could then be passed around by the guests at the dinner party. Alexander delivered, and on the 6th of December in 1810, Pintard eagerly showed off the two-paneled woodcut.

On the left was a portrait of Nicholas as a bishop, depicted as a leathery-faced, bald, and haloed gentleman with a tangled white beard, flourishing a birch rod in one hand, and a bulging sack of gold coins in the other. On the right was an image of two children, a well-kept young girl with a sweet smile ("the good child") and a crying boy with an untucked shirt and rumpled clothes ("the bad child"). The children were perched on the top of a crackling fireplace flanked by two stockings. The inscription underneath these images read:

"Saint Nicholas, my dear good friend!

To serve you ever was my end,

If you will, now, me something give,

I'll serve you ever while I live."

A fortnight later, the *New York Spectator* published a poem saluting the same, "good, holy man." Both the poem and the woodcut contained Easter eggs hinting at the traditions' Dutch origins, such as the oranges spotted in the stockings of the well-behaved child. This is believed to have been done in deference to the Orange-Nassau royals.

Pintard and Irving had successfully turned Saint Nicholas (and Sancte Claus), a former cult figure, into a household name, but his link to Christmas was still nonexistent. Christmas had been a fixture in the New World since the colonial era, but little was holy about its attached festivities. People wreaked cheerful havoc on the streets, utilizing the holiday as an excuse to consume barrels of liquor and drunkenly fire off their revolvers.

Both Pintard and Irving voiced their disapproval of the holiday, which had strayed away from its true meaning, on multiple occasions. Pintard, for one, insisted that it be restricted to a "family-oriented winter holiday for polite society." Irving parroted Pintard's sentiments in *Sketch Book*, published in 1819. By describing a family eating a scrumptious Christmas dinner, he was reinforcing and supporting the then-unpopular concept of a family-friendly celebration.

Minister Clement Clark Moore was pleased with the growing popularity of Saint Nicholas, but he was even more pleased when he stumbled upon an obvious, yet untrodden path. In 1823, Moore published "An Account of a Visit from Saint Nicholas," also published under "'Twas the Night Before Christmas." In this endearing poem, Moore purposely tied the arrival of Saint Nicholas to Christmas Eve, which he hoped would further validate the cause of Pintard and Irving.

Supposedly, Moore got his inspiration during a shopping outing in a sleigh, and he based his Santa Claus on a Dutchman who lived in Chelsea.

> "So up to the house-top the coursers they flew,
> With the sleigh full of toys, and Saint Nicholas too.
> And then, in a twinkling, I heard on the roof
> The prancing and pawing of each little hoof.
> As I drew in my hand, and was turning around,
> Down the chimney Saint Nicholas came with a bound.
> He was dressed all in fur, from his head to his foot,
> And his clothes were all tarnished with ashes and soot;
> A bundle of toys he had flung on his back,
> And he looked like a peddler just opening his pack.
> His eyes -- how they twinkled! his dimples how merry!
> His cheeks were like roses, his nose like a cherry!
> His droll little mouth was drawn up like a bow,
> And the beard of his chin was as white as the snow…"

Saint Nicholas was no longer a glowering, vindictive phantom in a perpetually foul mood, but rather a jovial, dimple-cheeked, and red-nosed old fellow with soft, shimmering eyes. Moore's interpretation of Saint Nicholas was merciful and sweet-tempered, equipped with a "round belly that shook like a bowl full of jelly" with every note of his musical laugh. Several other passages in the poem contain vivid descriptions of his appearance, and new details of his backstory were also disclosed.

From the following, one can gather that Saint Nicholas was small, no larger than an elf:

> "But a miniature sleigh, and eight tiny reindeer,
>
> With a little old driver, so lively and quick,
>
> I knew in a moment it must be Saint Nick!"

The names of Saint Nicholas' reindeer, as well as his landing and docking methods, were also revealed:

> "...And then, in a twinkling, I heard on the roof
>
> The prancing and pawing of each little hoof...
>
> And he whistled and shouted, and called them by name:
>
> 'Now, Dasher! Now, Dancer! Now, Prancer and Vixen!

On Comet! On, cupid! On, Donder and Blitzen!'"

In less than 20 years, the anonymous poem, freely reproduced in every newspaper in the winter season, was known throughout the United States, and from there it would spread to the rest of the English world. "Genteel New Yorkers embraced Moore´s homey, child-centered version of Christmas as if they had been doing it all their lives."[2]

Given the evident timelessness and international popularity of Santa Claus, one can only wonder what's in store for him in the future, but it seems certain that Santa and St. Nicholas will help keep the memory of each other alive for a long time.

Online Resources

Other books about Christmas by Charles River Editors

Other books about Christianity by Charles River Editors

Other books about Saint Nicholas on Amazon

Further Reading

Editors, N C. *Who Is Saint Nicholas?* 2017, www.stnicholascenter.org/pages/who-is-st-nicholas/. Accessed 12 Dec. 2018.

Pronechen, J. *19 Little-Remembered Facts About Saint Nicholas.* 5 Dec. 2016, www.ncregister.com/blog/joseph-pronechen/19-little-remembered-or-forgotten-things-about-st.-nicholas. Accessed 12 Dec. 2018.

Editors, L V. *Top 10 Facts about Saint Nicholas.* 14 Dec. 2007, listverse.com/2007/12/14/top-10-facts-about-saint-nicholas/. Accessed 12 Dec. 2018.

Editors, B C. *Saint Nicholas Biography.* 1 Apr. 2014, www.biography.com/people/st-nicholas-204635. Accessed 12 Dec. 2018.

Rabiipour, N. *Saint Nicholas: Facts and Legends.* 5 Dec. 2017, www.catholiccompany.com/getfed/st-nicholas-facts-legends/. Accessed 12 Dec. 2018.

Mandal, D. *Christmas Special: 8 Fascinating Things You Should Know About Saint Nicholas.* 23 Dec. 2015, www.realmofhistory.com/2015/12/23/8-fascinating-things-you-should-know-about-st-nicholas/. Accessed 12 Dec. 2018.

Editors, N C. *Saint Nicholas—Nearly Everybody's Saint!* 2017, www.stnicholascenter.org/pages/people/. Accessed 12 Dec. 2018.

---

[2] Ibid.

Editors, Y D. *Saint Nicholas Facts*. 2010, biography.yourdictionary.com/st-nicholas. Accessed 12 Dec. 2018.

Editors, E C. *Saint Nicholas*. 2004, www.encyclopedia.com/people/history/russian-soviet-and-cis-history-biographies/saint-nicholas. Accessed 12 Dec. 2018.

Morrow, C A. *Saint Nicholas: Fact or Fiction?* 2015, www.franciscanmedia.org/saint-nicholas-fact-or-fiction/. Accessed 12 Dec. 2018.

Editors, W M. *The Historical Saint Nicholas*. 4 Nov. 2016, web.archive.org/web/20071218221242/http://www.hymnsandcarolsofchristmas.com/santa/historical_st__nicholas3.htm. Accessed 12 Dec. 2018.

Editors, S N. *Saint Nicholas - Patron Saint*. 2013, stnicholaschurchnyc.org/saint-nicholas.html. Accessed 12 Dec. 2018.

Graves, D. *THE BODY OF SAINT NICHOLAS LAY IN MYRA*. 28 Apr. 2010, www.christianity.com/church/church-history/timeline/301-600/the-body-of-st-nicholas-lay-in-myra-11629662.html. Accessed 12 Dec. 2018.

Olsen, T. *The Real Saint Nicholas*. Aug. 2008, www.christianitytoday.com/history/2008/august/real-saint-nicholas.html. Accessed 12 Dec. 2018.

Maguire, D. *Experts Confirm That 'Santa's' Bone Fits the Right Timeline to Belong to St Nicholas*. 7 Dec. 2017, pickle.nine.com.au/2017/12/07/11/02/santa-bones-saint-nicholas-carbon-dated. Accessed 12 Dec. 2018.

Editors, N W. *Saint Nicholas*. 7 Aug. 2015, www.newworldencyclopedia.org/entry/Saint_Nicholas. Accessed 12 Dec. 2018.

Daley, J. *Is This St. Nicolas' Pelvis Bone?* 8 Dec. 2017, www.smithsonianmag.com/smart-news/bone-old-enough-be-santa-clauss-pelvis-180967444/. Accessed 12 Dec. 2018.

Editors, N C. *Was Saint Nicholas A Real Person?* 2005, www.stnicholascenter.org/pages/real-person/. Accessed 12 Dec. 2018.

Editors, N C. *Adam English: Digging Back to the Real Saint Nicholas*. 2 Dec. 2012, www.stnicholascenter.org/pages/adam-english/. Accessed 13 Dec. 2018.

Lendering, J. *Nicholas of Myra: Early Evidence*. 2017, www.stnicholascenter.org/pages/early-sources/. Accessed 13 Dec. 2018.

Editors, L. *Nicholas of Myra*. 23 Nov. 2018, www.livius.org/articles/person/nicholas-of-myra/?. Accessed 13 Dec. 2018.

Editors, N C. *The Real Face of Saint Nicholas*. 5 Dec. 2007, www.stnicholascenter.org/pages/real-face/. Accessed 13 Dec. 2018.

Norris, S T. *PLAGUE OF CYPRIAN: A PLAGUE BLAMED ON CHRISTIANITY*. 29 Dec. 2016, www.romeacrosseurope.com/?p=5891#sthash.cwal5D5L.XQht8Bzv.dpbs. Accessed 13 Dec. 2018.

Ciofarri, G. *Medieval Sourcebook: The Translation of Saint Nicholas (Greek Anonymous Account, 13th Cent. MS)*. Nov. 1997, sourcebooks.fordham.edu/basis/nicholas-bari.asp. Accessed 13 Dec. 2018.

Editors, N C. *Saint in Bari*. 2010, www.stnicholascenter.org/pages/saint-in-bari/. Accessed 13 Dec. 2018.

Editors, C U. *Who Was Saint Nicholas?* 6 Dec. 2015, news.campbell.edu/articles/who-was-st-nicholas/. Accessed 13 Dec. 2018.

Editors, N C. *Saint Nicholas Timeline*. 2017, www.stnicholascenter.org/pages/timeline/. Accessed 13 Dec. 2018.

de Voragine, J. *The Golden Legend: Here Beginneth the Life of S. Nicholas the Bishop*. Sept. 2000, www.stnicholascenter.org/pages/the-golden-legend/. Accessed 13 Dec. 2018.

Jones, C W. *The Life of Saint Nicholas the Wonderworker*. 2016, www.stnicholascenter.org/pages/symeon-the-metaphrast/. Accessed 13 Dec. 2018.

Sewell, B. *Life of Saint Nicholas*. 2009, www.stnicholascenter.org/pages/michael-the-archimandrite/. Accessed 13 Dec. 2018.

Jones, C W. *The Military Officers*. 2014, www.stnicholascenter.org/pages/istratelatis/. Accessed 13 Dec. 2018.

Jones, C W. *The Translation of Saint Nicholas, Confessor*. 2017, www.stnicholascenter.org/pages/translation-i/. Accessed 13 Dec. 2018.

Editors, N C. *Traditional Stories & Legends*. 2017, www.stnicholascenter.org/pages/traditional-stories/. Accessed 13 Dec. 2018.

Editors, N C. *Saint Nicholas Poems* . 2013, www.stnicholascenter.org/pages/poems0/. Accessed 13 Dec. 2018.

Editors, X U. *Saint Nicholas Day Quotes and Prayers*. 2018, www.xavier.edu/jesuitresource/online-resources/quote-archive1/st-nicholas-quotes. Accessed 13 Dec. 2018.

Editors, N C. *Nicholas's Birth**. 2017, www.stnicholascenter.org/pages/birth/. Accessed 13 Dec. 2018.

Editors, N C. *Boyhood: Tragedy Strikes*. 2015, www.stnicholascenter.org/pages/boyhood/. Accessed 13 Dec. 2018.

Editors, N C. *The First Miracle*. 2017, www.stnicholascenter.org/pages/first-miracle/. Accessed 13 Dec. 2018.

Editors, O C. *Saint Nicholas the Wonderworker and Archbishop of Myra in Lycia*. 6 Dec. 2016, oca.org/saints/lives/2016/12/06/103484-st-nicholas-the-wonderworker-and-archbishop-of-myra-in-lycia. Accessed 14 Dec. 2018.

Editors, S P. *Life of Saint Nicholas the Wonderworker*. 2016, www.spc.rs/eng/life_saint_nicholas_wonderworker. Accessed 14 Dec. 2018.

Vasilik, V. *A MIRACLE OF SAINT NICHOLAS*. 12 Dec. 2014, orthochristian.com/70898.html. Accessed 14 Dec. 2018.

Oliver, M. *10 Bizarre Stories About The Real Saint Nicholas*. 17 Dec. 2016, listverse.com/2016/12/17/10-bizarre-stories-about-the-real-saint-nicholas/. Accessed 14 Dec. 2018.

Editors, N C. *Three Impoverished Maidens or The Story of The Dowries*. 2017, www.stnicholascenter.org/pages/three-impoverished-maidens/. Accessed 14 Dec. 2018.

Editors, N C. *Pilgrimage to the Holy Land**. 2017, www.stnicholascenter.org/pages/pilgrimage-to-the-holy-land/. Accessed 14 Dec. 2018.

Editors, G. *Saint Nikòlaos De Bari, Bishop De Myra*. 24 May 2018, www.geni.com/people/Saint-Nikòlaos-de-Bari-Bishop-de-Myra/6000000007097847692. Accessed 14 Dec. 2018.

Editors, E W. *NICHOLAS ARCHBISHOP OF MYRA IN LYCIA*. 2015, www.ewtn.com/library/MARY/NICKLIFE.HTM. Accessed 14 Dec. 2018.

Editors, N C. *How Nicholas Became a Bishop*. 2016, www.stnicholascenter.org/pages/how-nicholas-became-a-bishop/. Accessed 15 Dec. 2018.

Editors, N C. *Fire Did Not Consume*. 2017, www.stnicholascenter.org/pages/fire-did-not-consume/. Accessed 14 Dec. 2018.

Dimitri, S. *The Life of Saint Nicholas the Wonderworker, Archbishop of Myra in Lycia*. 2018, www.stnicholasportsmouthnh.org/about/life-of-st.-nicholas-archbishop-of-myra. Accessed 14 Dec. 2018.

Ridgeway, J, and J Casella. *Santa Was in Prison and Jesus Got the Death Penalty*. 2017, www.stnicholascenter.org/pages/santa-prison/. Accessed 14 Dec. 2018.

Parker, J. *Persecuted, Jailed, Passionate*. 2003, www.stnicholascenter.org/pages/my-kind-of-santa/. Accessed 14 Dec. 2018.

Editors, P B. *Saint Nicholas: The Real Story of the Man Who Became Santa Claus*. 8 Dec. 2014, www.persecutionblog.com/2014/12/st-nicholas-a-persecuted-christian.html. Accessed 17 Dec. 2018.

Editors, C C. *Catholic Activity: Life and Legend of Saint Nicholas*. 2018, www.catholicculture.org/culture/liturgicalyear/activities/view.cfm?id=1213. Accessed 17 Dec. 2018.

Editors, E W. *SAINT NICHOLAS OF MYRA BISHOP, CONFESSOR C. 342*. 2017, www.ewtn.com/library/MARY/NICHOLAS.HTM. Accessed 17 Dec. 2018.

Elderman, B. *The Legend of Bishop Nicholas of Myra: A Telling by Eldrbarry:* 1996, www.eldrbarry.net/mous/saint/stnick.htm. Accessed 17 Dec. 2018.

Editors, C H. *What Was the Real Saint Nicholas Known For?* 25 Oct. 2012, www.timothypauljones.com/church-history-what-was-the-real-st-nicholas-known-for/. Accessed 17 Dec. 2018.

Editors, N C. *Bishop Nicholas Loses His Cool (At The Council of Nicaea)*. 2017, www.stnicholascenter.org/pages/bishop-nicholas-loses-his-cool/. Accessed 17 Dec. 2018.

Editors, N R. *Let's Stop Celebrating Saint Nicholas Punching Arius*. 6 Dec. 2016, www.ncregister.com/blog/steven-greydanus/lets-stop-celebrating-st.-nicholas-punching-arius. Accessed 17 Dec. 2018.

Editors, N C. *Nicholas and the Temple of Artemis*. 2017, www.stnicholascenter.org/pages/temple-of-artemis/. Accessed 17 Dec. 2018.

Editors, S J. *The Life of Saint Nicholas the Wonderworker*. 2016, www.saintjohnorthodox.org/Saint Nicholas Book 04 - Nicholas vs Artemis.pdf. Accessed 17 Dec. 2018.

Hakim, D. *POLES APART: NICHOLAS OF MYRA*. 23 Dec. 1996, www.washingtonpost.com/archive/lifestyle/1996/12/23/poles-apart-nicholas-of-myra/3d06d1c3-447f-4b66-ad37-66190232c24a/?noredirect=on&utm_term=.73a391fd6175. Accessed 17 Dec. 2018.

Damick, A S. *Saint Nicholas, Enemy of Demons*. 9 Dec. 2015, blogs.ancientfaith.com/roadsfromemmaus/2015/12/09/st-nicholas-enemy-of-demons/. Accessed 17 Dec. 2018.

Lazendorfer, J. *The Mysterious Case of Santa Claus's Leaking Bones*. 12 Dec. 2013, mentalfloss.com/article/54146/mysterious-case-santa-clauss-leaking-bones. Accessed 17 Dec. 2018.

Editors, H T. *DEMRE AND PATARA*. 2017, hometurkey.com/en/destinations/demre-and-patara. Accessed 17 Dec. 2018.

Editors, L T. *Myra*. 2017, www.lycianturkey.com/lycian_sites/myra.htm. Accessed 17 Dec. 2018.

Dodge, M M. *A Song for Saint Nicholas*. 2016, www.stnicholascenter.org/pages/poem-dodge/. Accessed 17 Dec. 2018.

Editors, N C. *The Evil Butcher*. 2017, www.stnicholascenter.org/pages/evil-innkeeper/. Accessed 17 Dec. 2018.

Editors, B N. *Saints (Un)Preserve Us: Saint Nicholas Resurrects Pickled Boys*. 2000, www.beliefnet.com/faiths/christianity/orthodox/2000/12/saints-unpreserve-us-st-nicholas-resurrects-pickled-boys.aspx. Accessed 17 Dec. 2018.

Editors, W A. *Saint Nicholas and the Three Male Youths*. Dec. 2011, wtfarthistory.com/post/13828316335/saint-nicholas-and-the-three-male-youths. Accessed 17 Dec. 2018.

Editors, T B. *Looking at Art: Saint Nicholas and the Boys in the Pickling Tub*. 27 Dec. 2009, timesbulletin.com/Content/News/News/Article/Looking-at-art-St-Nicholas-and-the-Boys-in-the-Pickling-Tub-/2/4/156409. Accessed 17 Dec. 2018.

Nugent, C. *Saint Nicholas Turns Two Thieves Away From a Life of Crime*. 4 Mar. 2017, holidappy.com/holidays/St_Nicholas_and_the_Two_Thieves. Accessed 17 Dec. 2018.

Editors, N C. *Dragon Charmer*. 2017, www.stnicholascenter.org/pages/dragon-charmer/. Accessed 17 Dec. 2018.

Editors, N C. *Famine Relief or The Miracle of the Grain*. 2017, www.stnicholascenter.org/pages/famine-relief/. Accessed 17 Dec. 2018.

Editors, O X. *Could Ancient Bones Suggest Santa Was Real?* 5 Dec. 2017, www.ox.ac.uk/news/2017-12-05-could-ancient-bones-suggest-santa-was-real. Accessed 17 Dec. 2018.

Free Books by Charles River Editors

We have brand new titles available for free most days of the week. To see which of our titles are currently free, click on this link.

Discounted Books by Charles River Editors

We have titles at a discount price of just 99 cents everyday. To see which of our titles are currently 99 cents, click on this link.

Made in the USA
Middletown, DE
07 December 2024